# Abram Berry –
## A North Dakota Legend

*Doreen Berry Frost*

Copyright © 2014 Doreen Berry Frost
All rights reserved.

ISBN: 1500789348
ISBN 13: 9781500789343
Library of Congress Control Number: 2014914357
CreateSpace Independent Publishing Platform
North Charleston, South Carolina

Her dreams, her reminiscences—portraying deep devotion:

Often when I said I heard
Songs and music in the wind and rain
And everything that stirred,
You tried to hear them too–
Let me ride again on my wild mustang
While the west wind ruffles my hair.

> From her book of poems,
> *Prairies and Palaces*
>
> Dorothy Berry de St. Clement
> Nutley, New Jersey
> March 7, 1879–June 24, 1984

# Acknowledgments

Thank you to my husband, Gary, my daughters, Denise and Natalie, and my son, Todd, for their support and faith in my ventures through the years.

My twin sister, Diana, and brother, Douglas, and their families for amusing me when I took things seriously. My grandchildren, Brittany, Sierra, Zac, Nicholas, Steven, Alyssa, and Todd, Jr., for your love and sweetness.

My dear extended family, the Randall's in New Hampshire, who mean so much to me. My cousins Karen, Keri, and their families; Robert and Nancy Frost, Carol (Frost) Knust and Gail (Frost) Nolan for supplying me with great stories and memoirs of our family; and all my talented cousins from and in New Jersey. With you in my life, I have so much to smile about. Blessings to you all, dear ones.

# Contents

I      Introduction ................................................................. ix

II     About the Author ........................................................ xi

Chapter One            The Taylor Hotel ............................................. 1

Chapter Two            Land Offices and Town Stores ................... 27

Chapter Three          The Sioux State ............................................ 51

Chapter Four           " *Vive le Percheronne*"
                                     Filly and the Gypsies .................................... 69

Chapter Five            The Tumbleweeds of North Dakota........... 75

Chapter Six             Hotel Dining Room
                                     Becomes a Theater....................................... 93

Chapter Seven          School Days in Taylor................................ 103

Chapter Eight           Hotel Proprietor Becomes
                                     a Land Baron.............................................. 123

Chapter Nine            Round House Engine – Ol' Brute............ 145

Chapter Ten            The A-BAR-B Ranch................................. 151

| Chapter Eleven | Cowgirls Go to New Jersey ......................... 167 |
| Chapter Twelve | Going Home to Teach School .................. 179 |
| Chapter Thirteen | Cowgirl to Countess ................................... 215 |

# Introduction

Dear Reader:

With an overflowing heart, I write this story. All of the memorable happenings that constitute the substance of this book actually took place in the world of reality on the lengthened lands of North Dakota, 1884. Every character in this story lived, breathed, and had his or her being on this gumbo soil on the outskirts of the Badlands.

This is not a history book, nor is it a book written to a set pattern. It is the story of the West, woven around a man who, ignoring organized religion, lived according to a personal creed that radiated in a wide circle and colored the lives of many people from the Red River Valley to the slopes of the Rio Grande. It is a challenge to the old American way of life. It is the spirit of the West, taking its last stand.

"Five years old and going out west! You're a wee tot to be so full of thrills and titters to see the Indians and outlaws!" Old Mose Adams put his hand on my head, and tears rolled down his cheeks as he looked at Maple and me, standing on the station platform in the quaint little town of Chester, New Jersey, that early spring morning. "Chester is a good little town, but I'm taking Maple and Dotty out to North Dakota—out to the great open spaces where they can grow up with freedom!"

"I've got another reason for going out west: here I am, *Abraham Bloomfield Berry*, twenty-five years old, but I'm not free! I am tied to my mother's apron strings; I'm tied to my father's suspenders and tied to my three sisters' pigtails. I'm the only boy in the family, and they all want to run my life. They wouldn't let me grow up when I put on long pants and started to shave. When I married Annie, I had to bring her home. They mean all right, but I want freedom! Now Annie and I are going out west to bring up our children according to the Bible. Some place in that good book it says, 'Bring up your children the way they must go, and they'll never depart from it.' My children must grow wings, and I'll never be the one to clip them!"

According to the memoirs of my great-aunt Dorothy Berry, beloved daughter of Abram and Annie Berry, her sister Maple Berry—my grandmother—married William J. Frost, her school sweetheart and a successful businessman from New Jersey, in 1902. Dorothy became a countess when she married the nobleman, Count Giulio de Sauteiron de St. Clement from the Castle of de Berthamond in Rome, Italy. She was a cowgirl and became a countess.

This is like a fairy tale, and perhaps boys and girls who read this book may find that their dreams can come true. Reading through these pages of their lives may awaken your imagination and cause you to question the greatness of your ancestors. Abram Berry was my great-grandfather. You may admire him too.

        Doreen Berry Frost, Author

# About the Author

Doreen Berry Frost is an author, vocalist, and retired entertainer from various Top 40 bands of the 1960s to the 1990s. Her past years as a recording artist came about from her dedicated studies in Boston at the New England Conservatory of Music and Boston University School of Fine Arts. She recorded an LPN record album in New York City for The Christian Science Publishing Society in Boston, Massachusetts, released in 1974 and titled "His Song Shall Be with Me," and her Dodie Frost Country Album, recorded in Nashville, TN, was released in 1982. She was a member of the American Guild of Variety Artists for thirty-five years.

When Doreen returned from recording in Nashville, her twin sister, Diana, called and told her that the city of Peabody had won the bid for the first women's world softball tournament to be held in the state. She said that they needed a jingle for advertising and a theme song for the Hall of Fame. Diana (an accomplished violinist and businesswoman) was the chairman of the entertainment committee for the chamber of commerce in Peabody, Massachusetts. This was when "Dodie Frost" wrote two song lyrics for the US Slo-Pitch Softball Association, headquartered in Petersburg, Virginia. Dodie immediately called the pianist and songwriter that she had worked with in Nashville, Beegie Adair, and asked if she would help her with this project. She responded, and the two songs, titled "Something is Happening at Cy Tenney Park" and "Give Me a Slo-Pitch" became souvenir records to support the chamber and to commemorate the event.

In 1999, Doreen and her husband, Gary LeBlanc, retired and moved to Florida. They loved the new life they had chosen: walking the beach, dining with new friends, and feeling a kinship with the tropical life around them—pelicans, dolphins, and birds of all types. It was energizing and encouraging discovering a wellspring of talent among the seniors in their circle of friends. Doreen published her first book under her stage name, Dodie Frost, coauthored with Donald O. Burling, USNR—he was ninety-nine years old at the time (2001)—titled *The Soldier, the Sailor, and the Singer*. (This book can be purchased online at www.amazon.com.)

**Note:** This book, *Abram Berry - A North Dakota Legend*, will educate all ages about the lives of those who loved, lived, and endured the times before the convenience of indoor plumbing, electricity, and paved roads. Reading books, homeschooling, and self-discipline instilled good social behavior, along with the hard work of homesteading, farming, and ranching, which resulted in success as the West expanded and grew.

*Chapter One -*
# The Taylor Hotel

Life in North Dakota nearing the turn of the century creates the setting for this story written around the life of Abraham Bloomfield Berry, one of the influential pioneers who showed the way in the Great Northwest. Father was a great man in his sincere honesty with people, with himself, and in his reasoning, but he was also purposeful in his thinking and quick acting on his decisions. He was not a great man in the marble-bust, leaded-glass-window, or Memorial Park sense of the word. He was a great man because he had the will and the courage to break away from many of the old and accepted beliefs of humankind and because he lived close and constant to the living sources of reality. He was a great man because, through his love of life, he accepted all the joy, humor, and wonderment created around him, and he reacted to the power, the presence, and the eminence of enchanted things that most adults usually grow away from. He was a great man because he retained his simple trusting faith in humanity in the face of the stern and homely visage of a wild and western world.

This is a story of my life with Father, Mother, and sister on those virgin prairies of the Great Northwest, where I grew up among the herds, the crops, the cowboys, and the Indians. [Note: the common term for **Native American** was, at the time of this story, **Indian**, and it is therefore the term used throughout the book.] Taylor, North Dakota, was not the gopher-mound town that we had expected to see but a wide-awake, booming treeless town that transacted more business in a day than Chester, New Jersey, did in a month. That was father's brief summary.

Our home, *The Taylor Hotel,* was on the corner of Main Street and Oak Avenue. North of us lay First, Second, Third, and Fifth

Streets. East of Oak Avenue lay Linden, Chestnut, and Vanier Avenues. West of us lay Elm, Ertel, and Dagmaull Avenues. The Northern Pacific Railroad paralleled Main Street with its track and sidetracks, and on the south side of the tracks was a small part of the town with Front Street and South Street and the Avenues still unnamed.

Outside of the named streets there were farms of 160 acres, some with well-built houses, and some held down by law with only shacks.

Father's letterheads described the town and incidentally drew attention to the hotel. The first set read, in large letters: "THE TAYLOR HOTEL"; under this, in small lettering: "Taylor is on the line of the Northern Pacific Railway, 565 miles west of St. Paul, and is situated in the midst of a superior farming and ranching community. A. B. Berry, Proprietor."

A more elaborate letterhead was used for prospective land buyers as father became, at once, a land agent for railroad and government lands. The letter's heading was in gold and red, and the description read: "TAYLOR is centrally located in Stark County, eighty miles west of the Missouri River, on the main line of the Northern Pacific Railroad. Its future prosperity is based on its rich agricultural resources, immediate tributary, and extensive stock ranges lying north and south in the Knife and Heart River Valleys. Choice railroad lands, with government claims adjoining, still to be had within five miles of town. All letters of inquiry, pertaining to land matters and hotel accommodations will receive prompt attention, by addressing A. B. Berry, Proprietor of the Taylor Hotel."

The Taylor Hotel was the largest building in town—with the exception of the wheat warehouse—and its grounds covered two lots. A large red barn with white trimmings stood at the far end. This was built like an Eastern barn: with stalls for horses and cows and feed bins and a loft above for hay. The front of the barn had rolling doors and room for a buggy and a runabout. There were other buildings and pens for chickens and turkeys and pigs, and there were times when Father was almost a farmer, or a commissioner man, selling the stock as it was brought in to him. Sometimes he would buy a "good bargain in stock," and sometimes he would take stock for a hotel debt, and very often he would buy a farm animal just because he liked to have a lot of live things around the place. "These are my sub humans," he would say, and he had a great understanding of animal nature and a love for animals that brought them close to humans.

Close to the back of the hotel was another building: a combination icehouse and cyclone cellar. This was built in a knoll, dug deep under the ground with the front doorway level with the ground and convenient for us to take shelter quickly when the twisters would come over the prairies, playing pranks with their vacuum funnels. Cyclones did not come very often, so we did not have to remain long on the straw-covered ice, but it was the safest place, just in case.

## The Privy

On the east side of the hotel stood a double building, well built with clapboards and trimmings and painted canary-yellow with green trim, just like the hotel. A cinder path led to it, and a latticed trellis hid the two doors. Over the right-hand door was "Ladies," and over the left-hand door was "Gents." This was our private and public privy, and the keys hung in back of the desk in the office so that the hotel guests had to ask for them. This privy was as clean and sanitary as water, soap, and lime could make it, and it was father's pride that no building of its kind in the Northwest could hold a candle to it. It was well stocked with old editions of the *Dickinson Press* and *St. Paul Daily* and the last discarded catalogs of Montgomery Ward and Company.

In the men's section there was often a picture on the wall from the *Police Gazette* of a strong man, prizefighter, and a girl in tights, famous for her buxom beauty in the burlesque shows. In the women's section, the selection of art was quite different. I remember one framed picture of "faith, hope, and charity" represented by three types of beauty: a blonde, a brunette, and a vivacious redhead. I distinctly recall another picture on that wall: a page taken from a magazine cover—a kitten playing with a ball of yarn. Many an artist has tried the subject, and it is fascinating. This kitten was entirely enmeshed, entangled, and wrapped in the unwound ball of yarn, and the innocent, questioning look in the kitten's eyes—human and appealing in its helplessness. Who had not found himself or herself, at some time or other, enmeshed in the web of life? Father said that he put that picture in there to create serious thinking for those who just sit and think.

In both sections of this outbuilding there was a three-holer: large, medium, and small. Matthias Trollop called it "The House of the Three Bares; the great big bare, the medium-sized bare, and the little teeny-weeny bare." Matthias was a buyer for a St. Paul fur house and stayed with us several months every year, buying pelts and furs from the trappers. He was one of those men with a misunderstood personality and a deep sense of humor, and he never laughed at his own or other people's jokes. Matthias liked to bet on everything and anything. Very often when he would see a man or woman walking on the cinder path toward the trellis, he would plank a quarter down on the table in the office and say, "I'll bet on the medium!" or "I'll bet on the large!" The cowboys would laughingly push his quarter back and say, "Can't bet with you, cuz ya can't prove it!" Then perhaps they would bet that the next man coming in the door would have spurs on, or, walking down the street, Matthias would bet, "The first greeting we hear will be 'Howdy!'" Wherever Matthias was, quarters were always passing back and forth in nonsensical bets.

The Taylor Hotel was not large as hotels run, and often it was not large enough to accommodate all the guests. The overflow would go to the section house across the tracks. The hotel had sixteen rooms, two stories with an attic and a cellar, and several outside sheds and storehouses. Father was not a hotel proprietor in the real sense of the word. He was always a host, welcoming his guests, paying and nonpaying alike, with a sincere smile, a handshake, and open-house hospitality. "I can't see a poor devil go hungry," he would say to mother as she would question him when a new face appeared at the table. "No, he can't pay me today, but I'll charge it on the books, and he'll bring me some livestock if he can't find the silver." This usually proved true, and with father's bookkeeping, he could make more fattening and selling the chickens, turkeys, and pigs and then give another "poor devil" a free meal and still have his books balance. So he was never in the "red."

Mother was not a hotel proprietress in the real sense of the word either. She was an excellent housekeeper and homemaker, and father gave her the degree of M.D.P.R.: "Manager of Domestic and Pecuniary Resources." She was careful, thrifty, and practical, with a disposition to save, and for this she felt grateful to a Scottish ancestor for a faint strain of Scottish blood. She would say, "If I was not thrifty, I don't know what would happen to us. Abie spends as if he always had the First National Bank back of him, and he never looks for a rainy day!"

Mother always had two girls to help her—capable strong Norwegian or Swede young women who could shoulder the burden of the work. Mother was a systematic manager, and there was a wholesome order about the hotel that made it attractive to guests who would be drawn to Taylor just to sleep in a good bed and enjoy an appetizing homey-like meal. Mother's cooking there was the same that she would do for her family: no skimping and no substitutes. "I only know one way to cook, and so I teach my girls."

Dinner was served at noon and supper in the evening at a long dining room table laid with a white linen cloth and linen napkins. If the table was not long enough to accommodate all, additional tables were added. Silver casters stood at each end of the table, with glass bottles of salt, pepper, vinegar, and mustard in shining clearness.

Father sat as host at the end of the long table, beaming on his guests, telling stories, making them all feel at home, and even making some of them eat more than they usually did. Mother would try to instill in his mind that this was a hotel and not a charitable institution. She would instruct, "Pass everything once and don't pass it again! Why, you urge everyone to have several helpings, and there go your profits!"

Abram would explain, "I can't carve a turkey or chicken that I have fed and raised myself on corn and wheat and then see these poor devils sit here with their tongues hanging out for another piece; and, I can't stop on one piece myself!"

"Oh, you know I don't mean to starve you, and none of you look starved! We are serving a fifty-cent dinner, so don't urge them to eat a dollars' worth." The fame of mother's cooking spread far and wide: roast chicken that even the South could not duplicate and hot biscuits, which father said sometimes burned on the top because they would puff up so light that they would hit the top of the oven. Every vegetable had a savory fragrance of its own flavor. They were not overcooked. Her pies were deep and luscious, and her cakes were mounds of delight.

Traveling men on the Northern Pacific would often stop off to have dinner and supper and stay overnight before going on to the county seat, just to enjoy all that our hotel had to offer them. It was more than the food and the bed that attracted the many guests who tarried under our roof. It was the peaceful harmony of a happy household and the sincerity of a welcome that reached to the heart and not to the pocketbook.

The Taylor Hotel had a homelike spirit, and it brought the East to the West. It was a refuge for the souls who were tired combating strife. Once, as a stranger/guest said good-bye to Mother, he took her hand, and tears were in his eyes: "This is the only home atmosphere I've ever known, Mrs. Berry, but I can't afford to stay any longer. Thank you for all your kindness. A father and a mother couldn't have done more!" He was trying to sell clocks, picture frames, and shelf ornaments made from the Florida-coast seashells, but he did not have enough sales appeal to put his goods over.

Mother noted his boyish look, and that he was run down at the heel, and it touched the soft spot in her heart, so she invited him to remain another week as her guest. Falls Ramsey accepted her invitation and stayed another week, and that put so much gumption in him that he sold all his ornaments, sent to Florida for more, and remained with us several months. Falls was a changed man from then on, with a new personality and a belief in himself and his own capabilities. He had found a man and woman who believed in him and trusted him to the extent of taking him in their home, so he could not let them down.

He conceived a new idea of selling his shell ornaments to the Western trade. Every Saturday night he held a raffle in the General Store, and he worked out many different schemes so his lottery was fair and square. Everyone who bought a ticket received a prize: they ranged from tiny shell pen wipers to thimble holders to large eight-day clocks, vases, umbrella stands, and footstools. Falls Ramsey established a business for himself, which grew until he and his agents covered the whole northwest. Every autumn he would return to our section of the country and be our guest for several months.

We always looked forward with pleasure to his return. He would come bounding up the front steps, rush in the door, throw his hat, grip, and cane anyplace they would land, and look for every one of us. Tall, thin, and lanky, he towered above us all and gave each one of us a hug with his long arms that seemed to wave around like an octopus. Then he would hold us out at arms' length and tell Father and Mother how good they looked and act surprised and awed that my sister Maple and I were always growing. Several times he came back from the kitchen with his face red, slapped by a new maid whom he had hugged before he looked. Nothing daunted Falls Ramsey. He was a success, and he radiated wholesome joy in serving the world with something that was not a necessity. But it was his reason for being because, through these articles of beauty and ornamentation, he had found himself. Father used to tell him, "We can't forget you, Ramsey, because this hotel is fairly wreaking with your gimcracks!"

Father and Mother had found their right niche in this world in the prairies of the West. This broad expanse of land and sky appealed to their love of freedom and expansion. Both of their natures were big and generous, and life was a privilege that they were grateful to live with a fullness of expression. Father accepted his place in the West as a challenge to leadership, and he was foremost in all civic and social activities. He was always working for the principles of right and justice and figuring on the basic good for the community while fighting against the western spirit, which was dominant, and where "might is right" had prevailed.

## Political Wisdom

Western politics was just like Eastern politics with business taking a decided boost or a decided slump before and sometimes after the election. Father was a radiating center of political wisdom at these times, and his magnetic personality could sway votes like a magic wand. Maple and I knew his stump speech by heart and would deliver it in front of our dolls and sometimes to the children we played with. We would swing our arms just like father and raise our voices: "Men of Stark County, I am not going to tell you how to vote! That would be going beyond the bounds of right and propriety! I am not as presumptuous as that! You are men of great minds and integrity!" (Maple and I would say, "You are men of 'tegrity!'")

Father would point to his men in the audience, and his words would ring true and sincere: "You are all big men, all high-minded enough to look past all personalities in this election! You can look past all sectional issues (Maple and I would say "sexual issues") or demands, all man-made platforms and policies!

"Men of Stark County, you must look past all purely political considerations and listen to that wee, small voice within yourself. That is your conscience talking to you. (Maple and I would say, "conscious talking to you") That is your best self! Men of the West, the Easterners have turned their faces westward to populate and develop this great and beautiful nation. We want to be men and stand on a platform of honesty and justice for all! Everyone who is listening to me—ranchers, farmers, cowboys, and gentlemen of the plains—you represent the government! You are the government! I am not going to tell you who to vote for because you have a mind of your own and a good mind to reason and judge, and I know that when you cast your ballot it will be in conformity with your intuitive reasoning!"

Father would make a sweeping bow, and after the applause he would shake hands, and sometimes a Democrat would call out, "What are you hollerin' about when I am goin' by?"

"Humph!" said father. "What are you going by for when I am hollerin'?"

Then he would fling back with a laugh, "Just a little common sense talk, which you wouldn't understand!"

The setting for father's platform speech was always carefully laid out with pictures of his candidates under the American flag and well-worded campaign slogans in clear view. On his coat lapels he had all the badges and buttons of his side, and sometimes the name of his highest candidate was on his hat. His political psychology worked wonders and did more to turn Democrats into Republicans than any other influence in Stark County.

While he was a political leader and put his heart and soul into keeping local politics clean, he never ran for any state office, even if Mose Adams of Chester, New Jersey, had prophesied, "You're the kind of timber for the legislate, Abie. You've got book learnin', an' you're right smart lookin' too! You got a way o' makin' folks beli'vin' what you say! I know you'll be settin' in one o' them high-back chairs in Washington someday—then you'll remember Ole' Mose!"

Father aspired to only two local offices: president of the county school board and justice of the peace of Stark County. With these two offices he could appoint high-grade school teachers from the East and give the children of the small-grade schools equal advantages, and he could see that law and justice were carried out in his community. I used to talk about it in general: "Papakins raises pigs for politics!" because I had heard him say, "All of my hog money goes for politics, and it takes a damn lot of hogs to keep us out of the mire! Hogs are clean too—the cleanest animals there is. They wouldn't live in mud and filth unless humans made them. Why, not one of my hogs would wallow in this quagmire of political mud that is seething all over the country at election time! If my hogs won't wallow in it, I'll be damned if I will! I will do my level best to keep my feet and the feet of my candidates on a sandbar if we can't reach an anchored rock!"

My childish impression of politics was rather confusing; Republicans and Democrats meant good people and bad people. Because we had a Republican community and a strong Republican state, I did not hear any good about the Democrats, so I formed my own conclusions. My ideas became more set when an Indiana minister and his family stopped at the hotel for a few weeks during a heated campaign. His ten-year-old son sang: "Democrats, eat dead rats!" There were more jingles too terrible to mention, and Mother forbade us to listen to him, but I decided it was better to be a "dirty Republican" than a "rotten Democrat." My best and foremost conclusion was in favor of Republicans because Father was a Republican, and Father was always right.

I have vivid recollections of father as a justice of the peace. He would hold court at various places to suit the convenience of the parties involved. Father's business was always our business; he had a way of bringing home all the highlights of what happened, dramatizing it and making it more interesting, more tragic, or more humorous.

An insignificant little incident, told by my father, assumed the aspect of a thrilling adventure. Our bedtime stories were always true stories; at least they were built around one true fact that was tangible.

One of his stories included the life of a great man who struggled with ill health—poor eyesight and asthma. His family was wealthy, so he was educated at home by tutors. His poor health concerned him; so his father set up a gymnasium in their home to help with his physical self-improvement.

This gentleman had a viewpoint of honesty and determination to stand for justice for the public good. He crusaded on all matters of American interest and particularly in the area of conservation. He spoke out to preserve our national forests here in the West and reserved land for public use—as long as no one littered or left the grounds disturbed. He assisted with great irrigation projects for our state. Father said that he rode right through Taylor, heading west to Medora, many times. There was great sadness in this man's heart. His wife, Alice, delivered a baby girl on February 12, 1884 while he was away at the assembly in Albany, New York, giving a speech. A telegram was sent to him of congratulations, and a roaring cheer filled the hall. A few hours later a second telegram arrived, instructing him to return home to New York City immediately. He rushed home in time to see his dear wife suffering from kidney failure—from complications at childbirth. Alice died two days later. The sadness escalated because his mother died from typhoid fever just hours before his wife—on the same day and in the same house. What strength this man had because he had been with both his wife and mother in their last hours.

"Father," I asked, "who is the man in the story? And is this a true story?"

Father leaned over both Maple and me with tears in his eyes, and he said, "Yes, this is true. It is Teddy, the man who bought a cattle ranch over in Medora in the Badlands of our Dakota Territory. He is grief stricken. He finds strength and some solace driving cattle and riding out on the open range."

Dotty asked again, "Who is he?"

Father's voice was soft, and he spoke with a raspy sound, like there was a frog in his throat. "He is the youngest president in our nation's history. He is *Theodore Roosevelt.*" And father continued, "When Teddy comes through his grief, you'll see that he will accomplish many things in his life. He is a strong and powerful speaker and leader for our country."

"I am a justice, a magistrate of the peace!" Father would say. "I'll vindicate and defend the righteous and just and see that the ornery ones get what they have brought upon themselves!"

One case in Father's court received a great deal of publicity and was given the front page in the New Jersey newspapers. Jim LaRue, a five-foot, side-warped, French Canadian, whose brain matter barely functioned, had stolen government blankets from the Indian reservation and had sold them across the border. Jim had made several successful trips and had come back for his last load when the deputy sheriff caught him with the goods: ten new blankets strapped under the saddles of his packhorses. Each blanket was stamped in blue lettering, "U.S."

I remember the night the sheriff brought Jim into the hotel. The little shriveled-up man was so frightened that he shivered and whimpered like a puppy afraid of punishment—just like our little Emil when he wet the floor and knew that Mother was going to stick his nose in it.

Father held court in the barn that day: the big doors were rolled up, and the buggy and runabout were outside. A big dry-goods box made a desk for Father, and with nail kegs, beer kegs and planks, there were seats for everyone who was present.

The trial had to be held in the barn because Jim LaRue's horses had to be present; they carried the evidence on their backs. Poor Jim! His lawyer was a big burley man with spectacles who towered above him and bent over as if he were peering at Jim through a microscope. Jim could not read or write; that is why his English was smattered with French. When he got on the stand (which was a soapbox), he could only blubber and wipe his nose with his fingers and keep repeating: "My blanket, my blanket! US Jim LaRue! My blanket! Jim LaRue, US."

With all the evidence against him—and even the Indians there to claim their blankets—still other thefts were heaped upon him. Jim persisted to claim that the initials stood for Jim LaRue. It was just like pronouncing sentence upon our puppy Emil as Jim's mind could not function any deeper. "Why put an imbecile in jail?" said Father. "But his imbecility turns to craftiness when it comes to theft! Poor devil, he's got to learn his lesson now; otherwise he'll go back to stealing!" Jim had to go to jail in Dickinson, the county seat.

I remember that evening: the sheriff, the lawyers, and some of the witnesses had supper at the hotel before taking the train for Dickinson. Jim was out in the barn with handcuffs on, and a deputy was left there to watch him. Mother told Nora to have one of the Norwegian girls take a plate of supper out to him. Nora begged, "Please don't ask me, Mrs. Berry, I can't do it—the dirty thief!"

Mother only said, "All right, Nora, don't do it!" Here was our chance. Maple and I were only too glad to do something for the pitiful little man, even if he was bad. Maple carried a plate of hot food, and I carried a cup of coffee, and his wizened face was expressionless when we brought it to him. The deputy took off his handcuffs, and we put the plate and cup on another box before him. Jim's little side-twisted body bent over it, and he used his knife to shovel in his food.

He ate so fast that we thought he was going to throw up, so Maple said, "Please, Mr. LaRue, don't hurry. You have lots of time before they take you to jail!" Then I put in what I had heard Father say, "Be a nice, good man, and you'll get out sooner!"

He had not noticed us before, but then he stopped eating with his knife blade heaped with creamed potatoes, poised halfway to his open mouth, and looked at us. "Huh! I no mister; I US

Jim LaRue! I'm always a good nice man! My blanket—no Indian blanket!" They took him to jail, and Father had great pity for him then, but later his conscience told him that he had done absolutely right. It was soon proven that Jim had stolen his horses and his saddles and all that he owned. He was a notorious thief and was wanted by the Canadian police. He finally landed in a Manitoba prison, and the horse thieving would put him in there for life. Father always considered his judgeship in a very serious light. He would say, "No one would need a justice of the peace if they lived right and was honest with themselves! Neither would they need lawyers, ministers, or doctors, who are only true to the ideals of their professions when they try to eliminate themselves, and how many do that?"

The most unusual cases came to Father's court, and as Father was quick to see the humorous side and bring it home to us, they stand out in my memory, while the long, serious cases excited little interest in our home. There was the case where Hank Bauer had sued Yan Jensen for ninety-nine dollars and had repeatedly been given Ian's note and a letter of explanation. Hank presented all the letters, and Father brought them home to read them before handling the case. One read, "I wish to pay you, but I am like you now. I am poorer than the devil—just like you. I send my note." Another letter: "I pay you when I raise the money, but you shall have it coming to you, which will make you glad!" Another letter, "I always tell you I pay you and don't take the bankruptcy law, which would cheat you. I send my note!" The last letter after five notes read, "You stop writing me a snotty letter. You say you sue me, but you lose your shirt then. We are both poor as the devil, so we cannot fight with lawyers. I only send note!" I think Father had to dismiss this case as Yan never had enough money to pay Hank, and with his renewed notes he hoped it would be settled someday.

Another time a cowboy from a Montana ranch burst into Taylor on his bronco and scared everybody by firing up in the air with his two guns. He did not hurt anyone, but the town was in an upheaval, and gossip had it that he had gone loco and was shooting to kill. The sheriff brought him in the hotel, and Father kept him for the night, put him in a room and in bed, and took his clothes away. The next morning the cowboy walked out as meek as a jackrabbit in his underwear and was full of apologies, but he had been arrested and had to have his trial. Abram fined him twenty-five dollars and the costs of court and also for the destruction of a sign post, the barber pole and several weather vanes—all shot full of holes with his crack marksmanship.

A cowboy from Nebraska had been working on a Montana cattle ranch for a year, and this was his first vacation. He admitted that he was not used to drinking whiskey, and a few drinks sent him completely loco, but he only meant to have a good time. He had a bag of silver in his saddlebags and counted out twenty-five silver dollars to pay his fine. Maple and I stood there gapping, and then he turned toward us and handed each one of us a silver dollar. "Here, girlies, buy yourself some hair ribbons! I have a little sister in Nebraska, and she wears big bows in her hair just like you!" He was our ideal of what a perfect cowboy should be in looks and behavior.

Many arguments and disputes came to Father to be settled, and he would usually take them to a corner of the dining room to talk it over. Next we would see two men walking out of the front door with their arms around each other and going to the Blind Pig Saloon to get a drink of rotgut. Or perhaps this time for some sarsaparilla, which is a carbonated drink flavored with dried fragrant roots. Father always said that when justice was one thing and law was another, he resorted to justice and considered that there was no reason for some of the rules in technical law.

There was the time when Mrs. Fulson, a retired schoolteacher from Illinois, came in to ask Father's advice. She wanted to raise horses on her ranch. How many geldings should she buy? "Don't buy any geldings," said Father, "but look that word up in your dictionary and buy brood mares."

"Oh, I have eight female horses; I guess they are mares. But I want a husband for them."

"Buy a stallion, Mrs. Fulson. But you had better wait until your son comes here from college, and he will be able to set you right on the sex of equine animals. He will also have to know what breed of horses he wants to raise."

Mrs. Fulson put on her schoolteacher air, "I know the breed, and I want to raise pintos!"

Father said he took about two hours of unpaid time to explain to Mrs. Fulson that a pinto was a piebald animal of variously mottled color and usually of mixed breeds, and those that she had admired so much were geldings. He finally persuaded her to let her son, Ralph, take responsibility for horse breeding on the ranch, and that he would help him in the choice of stock. Father's comment was, "Mrs. Fulson may be a good teacher of readin', learnin', and 'rithmetic, but she lacks understanding of animal husbandry."

Most of Abram's justice cases were fights of what he called his "hard liquor cases." From my memory it seems that North Dakota was always a prohibition state, and the "firewater" smuggled into the state was of the potency of wood alcohol. It was vile stuff and crazed men's brains more than other alcoholic drinks. A few drinks gave them laughing jags, and the next stage seemed to be the embraceable, brotherly love jag, where they fell all over each other and would swear a bond of everlasting friendship or swear to give each other all that they owned.

A little more drinking would bring on the singing stage. It was not "Sweet Adeline" in North Dakota but a folk song of whatever country the drunk persons came from. They could not get together with harmony, but they would all sing together: a Norwegian, Swede, German, Hungarian, Russian, Islander, Holland Dutchman, Irishman, Englishman, and sometimes there were French Canadians and Italians, but they were very few in that section. In the next stage of drinking, they would exalt the grandeur, wonders, and superior advantages of their particular countries. If there was any more drinking after that, it would result in a free-for-all fight or a fight between the parties who had called each other liars.

The justice of the peace office was a busy place on holidays or auction days or any day, which drew a crowd of farmers and ranchers and outsiders to the little town of Taylor. The sheriff would arrest the fighters, and Father would usually wait until they were sober and then give them a little oratory about disturbing the peace of this decorous community. They would pay their fine and swear that they would not touch "rotgut" whiskey again, and some of them kept their promise.

## Matrimonial Services

Berry, as justice of the peace had the authority to marry couples, but this rarely happened in this foreign-populated community. Marriage was a sacred rite and demanded a long ceremony by a minister or priest and a big celebration, which included friends for miles around. I can recall Father performing several marriages, and he performed them with great dignity and impressiveness. He dressed up with his black long-tailed coat, with stiff white cuffs showing and a Piccadilly collar. One end of our large dining room was a sort of sitting room and was cozily furnished with a large rug, a fashionable pillow-at-one-end couch, an upright organ, several rockers and chairs, a table with a tapestry tablecloth and table lamp on it, and china bric-a-brac.

Mother and Father made a great effort to decorate this part of the room for his marriage ceremonies. He would have flowers (real or artificial) on the table and organ and would hire someone to play the wedding march. The bride and groom would march in from the hall. Mother, Maple, and I and our Norwegian girls and some of the guests in the hotel would be the smiling witnesses and found it a home-like atmosphere. Maple said that I used to enjoy it so much that we longed for lots of weddings. We would even suggest to any man we knew if he was interested in some girl, "Let Father marry you. He'll do it quick and easy. He says, 'It's cheaper for two to live than one!'"

Father said, "When I splice them, I tie a surgical knot that encircles them and holds them for life." One couple that Father spliced was Durk and Ida. Durk was a telegraph operator and station agent for the Northern Pacific Railroad. He was a tall, gawky young man, and this was his first job away from home. He lived in the station, at one end of a long flat building, which had a platform all the way around it. He had three large rooms. Durk said, "I really don't live there; I jus' drag out my life there."

This was quite true as he made no effort to turn those three rooms into a home. A bed stood in the middle of one room, and one chair and a table were pushed about for convenience. They were usually littered with papers and magazines. The other two rooms were strewn with horse blankets, a saddle and bridle, and other horse accessories. He had to sleep in the station to be on duty when the night trains arrived, but all of his spare time he stayed at the hotel and took his meals with us. Father took him under his wing and treated him like a son, and Mother did his mending when his laundry came in. She said that she had to do this, or he would go around with his toes and elbows poking out because Durk did not care about clothes or how he looked. It was Father who told him to get married: "You need a wife, Durk, because you bob around here like a ship without a captain! You need a good little woman to manage your life for you. I can't be bothered with your petty responsibilities!"

Durk thought of his little country school sweetheart back on the farm near Elkhart, Indiana. "She was mighty sweet to me, and when I left, she promised to wait and marry me when I made my fortune in the West. I have in no wise made a fortune, but maybe she'll take me for the worse instead of the better! I've got enough money saved to furnish those three big rooms, and Ida is like her mother: she can make any place a home!"

That was all that Father needed to start the flame burning, and love is a powerful agent when it has susceptible hearts to work upon. Father, Mother, Maple, and I all took a keen interest in Durk's growing love affair. All of us read his letters from Ida like an open book. Father told him what to tell Ida; in fact, sometimes, Father would write the whole letter, and Durk would copy it. He said Durk's letters were too cold and commonplace and would never win a girl's heart. In two months this love affair came to a climax, and Ida arrived in Taylor to marry Durk.

In the meantime, Durk had tossed a lot of new furniture in his three rooms and had them thoroughly cleaned, which started some gossip, but no one knew the truth. When Ida arrived, Father met the train and walked with her to the hotel, and then the Taylorites did ask questions: "Who is she?" "Where did she come from?" and "What is she doing here?"

To all of this Father made only one reply: "My polite breeding forbids me to ask such impertinent questions of a young lady over eighteen! She may be the governor's daughter, for all I know!" Soon the story went around that the governor's daughter was staying at the hotel. This was great; it took all gossip away from Durk and his new furniture.

The wedding was very quiet and secretive because Durk could not be absent from the station for a honeymoon. Durk and Ida stood in our reception room corner of the dining room while Father tied his nonslipping surgical knot and pronounced them man and wife. We had a wedding supper that evening in the little back room off the kitchen so that the hotel guests would not learn the truth and serenade the bridal couple. Durk walked to the station as usual, and when it was very dark, Father and Mother escorted Ida to her new home.

It was two days before the secret leaked out, and that night there was a big serenade on the station platform. Ida said that she had expected it, so she had prepared a triple batch of cookies. She looked like a china doll when she came to the door and invited the serenaders in. Durk came out of the office and helped her make coffee. He was proud to present her to the Taylorites: "This is the little woman who will manage my life for me! When you want to deal with me, boys, you will have to deal with this little woman first!"

Another wedding stands out in my memory, but this one had a sordid background. It was a cold October day when Tad Bostrom brought his son Knute into the hotel at the point of a gun and made him marry little lame Tilly Jansen.

Tilly's "Paw" was there, too, with a gun on his hip to see that Knute did right by his daughter. Poor little Tilly looked so weak and pale because she was crying and frightened. She had her baby, and it came as a complete surprise to her family. It seems that she had helped to work on the farm all summer with her figure so bound up that her parents did not notice the rounded-out lines of maternity. Every detail of her life was so regulated and dictated by her parents that Tilly could not act for herself.

When it was time for her baby to be born, Tilly was frantic. She could not get away, so she hid in the barn in the haymow, and it was there that her father found her unconscious and moaning. Both she and the baby nearly died, but the spark of life held on, fighting to live, and won. Word came to Taylor that she was dying, and Father telegraphed to Dickinson, the county seat, for Dr. Stickney. That dear doctor rode twenty-three miles on horseback to try to save her life. The doctor stayed until Tilly and her baby were out of danger.

Knute Bostrom was in Montana, working on a cattle ranch. He came home as soon as his father called him. "Yes, it must be my baby," he said. "Tilly belongs to me only; but I never knew there was a baby!" Tad Bostrom cussed and swore at his son, calling him every name he could think of pertaining to the devil. The baby was born out of wedlock, and that was a terrible sin. They would not let Knute go to Tilly. Both fathers watched their children until Tilly was strong enough to travel to Taylor. Then they brought them in to father like lambs brought to a slaughter.

It was a pitiful situation until father turned on them. "I don't marry anyone behind a gun!" Then he took the two guns out in the office. "Now, Tad Bostrom and Paw Jansen, why are you condemning your own children—your own flesh and blood? The only crime I can see here is you two men threatening your children with guns!" Then Father turned to the two children—Knute was seventeen, and Tilly was only fifteen—"Do you two love each other?" They both nodded their heads and sobbed, "Yes!" Then he added, "Do you want to be legally married and raise that beautiful little boy to be a good citizen?" Again both nodded and sobbed "Yes!"

Father walked up to them and took their hands. "Now I know all about your story. You are too young, so your parents would not have agreed to a marriage. They are to blame more than you! There is no shame resting on the head of your blessed baby! No crime has been committed! These few words, which I will speak, cannot bind you closer than the vows you have made to each other! Now these overanxious fathers have provided the license, so all is ready." Knute and Tilly were looking into each other's eyes, smiling as father securely tied his unbreakable surgical knot of matrimony.

Another wedding is rather vague in my memory. The bride was from a "matrimonial bureau" and had been corresponding with Jasper Quill for over a year. Jas had written a lot of lies about his great rancho in North Dakota. He had pictured himself as a man of great wealth with thousands of acres of land, thousands of head of cattle and blooded horses, and an army of employees to look after his possessions. He described his ranch home as a mansion with all the modern improvements that could be brought to the plains.

Allie Leeman was a schoolteacher in Eldorado, Kansas. She had poured out her heart with sincerity in her letters to Jasper. She never doubted for a moment that his letters were not as truthful and sincere as they seemed. Jasper had asked her to marry him but had never set a date. He always seemed to have a vague excuse to postpone "the day that will give me something more valuable and precious than my material possessions!" Now the time had come when Allie had to make a great decision: either to sign a contract for a higher-salaried position in another school or marry Jasper. If she were going to marry Jasper Quill, why not do it at once while there was an easy chance to break away from school teaching? Allie asked herself this question, pondered over it, and then decided to go to Taylor, North Dakota, to see if she really wanted to marry this young man whom she had only known through his letters. They had exchanged photographs, and he had said, "You are just like the girl of my dreams!" She could have said the same and even more; there was so much strength of character and frank determination in his rather boyish face. He was rather young to be so wealthy and to have made it all by himself, even if such things could happen in a western country.

Allie arrived in Taylor on a hot day in August. Father was not at the station, but Falls Ramsey arrived on the same train with a new supply of gimcracks, and he escorted her to the hotel. She had asked Falls and now she asked Father how she could get out to Jasper Quill's ranch. They both told her there was no easy way, and no neighbor who lived near him was in town that day, but they would watch out for someone who was going in that direction. Allie had to stay at the hotel three days before an opportunity came for her to ride to Halliday, a distance of some thirty miles.

In the meantime, she had told her story to Mother. Mother read some of Jasper's letters, and then father was brought in to consider her confidence. Maple and I were in it, too, because nothing seemed to be secret in our home. We all accepted the facts as they made themselves plain and real. We knew Jasper well; when he came in from his ranch, he made himself perfectly at home at the hotel, even to the point of sitting in the kitchen, chatting with mother and the girls. He lived up in the clouds, building air castles. He owned 160 acres of government land and had built some kind of a shack on it. By hard work and thrift, he had accumulated some cattle, horses, and farm implements and had been trying both farming and ranching with fairly good success. He had great ambitions, and in his letters to Allie, he had pictured all of his plans coming true.

One of his common expressions was, "At the rate I'm going now, when I'm forty years old, I'll be worth forty thousand dollars!"

Then Father would chime in, "You can't tell by that. Why, at the rate I'm going now, with all my deadbeats, when I'm forty years old, I'll be in the poorhouse!" That was the character of Jasper Quill. Father and Mother told Allie the truth without disparaging the character of a fine young man. Father explained, "He is always rich in his mind, and he always will be! Go out and see him and don't act surprised. If you find that you can love him as he is and live on the ranch and help him to make his millions, marry him. If you can't do this, Miss Leeman, tell him so and go back to school teaching."

Allie did just as Father told her. Jasper was so happy when he saw her arrive that he forgot he had told her such whopping lies about his ranch. Allie saw great possibilities of making the ranch house something like his ideal and perhaps making all of his dreams come true. Jasper and Allie came back together, and Father trimmed up the dining room corner for the wedding ceremony. Mother planned a sumptuous wedding breakfast, and after Father had tied a cast iron, riveted surgical knot, they took the train for Dickinson to spend their honeymoon in our metropolis, "The Gateway to the West" and the scenic wonderland of the Badlands.

Dorothy Berry and Calico – 1895

*Chapter Two -*
# Land Offices and Town Stores

North Dakota was always considered just a bread-and-butter state, with nary a millionaire and nary a pauper. Families were leaving the crowded towns and farms of the central western states for the rich, low-priced lands or free homesteads where they were assured of big crops, free coal, and health, happiness, and fortune. The land offices of North Dakota did a flourishing business with their Western idea of advertising. It would run like this:

"There is always money in sight!" "We live in a God-blessed country and have only to take advantage of the opportunities at our very doorstep to become prosperous and rich and give our children a heritage worth having in a country worth living in."

A farmer newspaper came out with headlines, "Eastern and Western States, take notice. We're pretty comfortable here in North Dakota, thank you!" Once, after a very bountiful harvest, our self-advertising ran, "We have every reason for saying 'Aye, Aye!' to the next Thanksgiving proclamation, which the president can't put on any too strong to suit us!"

One land office kept a "sunshine table" for four years, proving that North Dakota had more hours of sunshine than any other state in the Union, and with sunshine, moisture and "elbow grease" and soil that has every element that nature gave it could only bring bonanza results. "The bounty of the soil is generous to those who hustle" was one good slogan that could not be denied.

"Free homestead for every family!" was the bait that brought home-loving men and women to North Dakota. They could secure title to a 160-acre tract of land under the government homestead law. After residing four and a half years, they could prove up and obtain title by paying the US Land Office two dollars and fifty cents per acre.

Any unmarried woman of age could enjoy the benefits of this homestead law, and all the sons and daughters of a family, after they had reached the age of twenty-one, were entitled to take up land. One land agent advertised: "Raise a family in North Dakota and become a land baron!" And it was quite true that large families of grown children owned hundreds of acres of free land for ranching and farming. Father used to say that the people who came to North Dakota had lots of heart, courage, and steel rods in their backbones. If they could not make a success of their homestead, they certainly could not blame the land for their own shortcomings for not a thing had been left out by nature. "Yes, sir-ree!" said Father; "it behooves every last man out here to be everlastingly up and hustling to keep pace with the sunshine and weather."

I can remember seeing men sitting around Father in the office, with broken pieces of lead pencils in their grimy fingers, "figgerin" on a piece of wrapping paper how much they had made on their different crops. One farmer would say, "The figgers look all right; the land is all right; but I ain't got any money! I must get a bigger slice of land, or I ain't got any percent!"

Abram gave him an eye survey: "Well, considering that you and your family do all your own work and that you raised your seed last year, I should say that you had 100 percent profit!"

The real estate men in North Dakota were "booming" the state, and sometimes it would be some particular town or section. "Booming" in the West was an art, requiring a little money, a great deal of printer's ink, and no end of push, "nerve," and "cheek!" The object of a "boom" was to attract settlers, advance the price if possible, and promote speculation. Many a "boom town" sprung up overnight as people sold their possessions to come west and grasp this golden opportunity to own land and a home and live close to nature in a God-favored country.

One real estate firm in Chicago who dealt in North Dakota land sent this circular through eastern and western states: "We have anything you want and at any price. We can sell you a city or a country home, and, if you ever come near, or within half a block of our office, we will do it, and I swear it! The preachers will look after your moral and spiritual welfare, but we will take care of your temporal affairs. If you come our way, it shall never be said (when the final settlement is made) that you were like one of the foolish virgins of old who wrapped her dough in a handkerchief and sank it in a well. On the contrary, your record shall be that of the good husbandman who put his wheat in good Red River Valley soil, and it produced a thousand fold, and it came to pass that he, who had nothing (but faith in us) had more ducats than he knew what to do with."

Another real estate dealer with a flair for rhyme and reason sent out very attractive circulars with this rhymed heading:

> No Other Land, No Other Clime on Top of God's Green Earth
> Where Land is free as Church Bells Chime Save the Land of Dakota Dirt
> Here, for a Year of Honest Toil a Home You May Insure
> And from the Black and Loamy Soil a Title in Fee Mature
> No Money Needed Until the Day When the Earth Itself Provides
> Until you Raise a Crop No Pay—What Can You ask Besides?

This was skillful "booming," and it had that peculiar social flavor of the energetic West. The Western business creates a chummy atmosphere, which is as true today as it was then. It is that free, bounding spirit of the prairies that makes "the sun a little brighter, the sky a trifle bluer, and friendships a trifle truer."

There was a hustling real estate office in the little town of Richardton, five miles east of Taylor, where they published a farm paper, and their advertising was unique and amusing. Father saved many of the old copies. One land "booming" article read thus: "A Philadelphia poetess sings: 'I would not weep because the roses die.' Why, no indeedy, that is nothing to cry about. But if you do not buy North Dakota land while it is cheap, then you had better lift up your voice and howl till they can hear you in Nevada."

This article appeared in the same paper:

> As the rain is said to descend alike upon the just and the unjust, we had begun to fear that our people were neither just nor unjust, as all the rains seemed to avoid us; but on Sunday afternoon last, the heavens opened, and a most lovely rain was the result; and now we hope to see more people in our midst ready to take advantage of our Land Bargains, for our price of ten dollars to eighteen dollars an acre will soon cease to be quoted.

Another issue of the Richardton paper had this "booming" article:

> He who makes two blades of' grass grow where one grew before, is a benefactor to his race." Far be it for us to write a more beautiful or truer sentence so we only add that everyman or woman who buys an acre of North Dakota land is a benefactor to his true race!

In this same issue one of my poems was published, titled "Dakota Land." I had the flare for rhyming, and Father encouraged it by giving me titles and suggestion on subjects to write about. I was very proud when I saw my first poem in a newspaper, and then I looked for the check to arrive. My poem had been accepted. I must receive some compensation, and I insisted that Father inquire of the editor.

Father did consider that this was important, and while in Richardton he stopped in at the newspaper office. That worked. I received a very businesslike letter from the editor, thanking me for the "beautiful poem that praised North Dakota so sincerely." A check for one dollar on a Mandan Bank was enclosed, and this first dollar made by my own efforts, had the value of a million in my childlike eyes. Many years after this, I learned that Father went to the editor and left a silver dollar on his desk to pay me for the poem, saying, "You better pay my daughter something for her poem 'Dakota Land,' or she is liable to write another poem on 'Dakota Drought.'" And there is much that could be written on that.

### DAKOTA LAND
#### by Dotty Berry (age nine)

Why don't you come to Dakota, This land so fair and free?
It's the land that suits the people, and it's the land for me!
Its beautiful hills and valleys, Prairies that wave and roll;
Ravines and canyons and gullies where lurks the coyote bold.
Here is rich and fertile land that yields to plow and hoe;
Grass that makes the best of hay, and farmers love to mow.
The grass that fed the buffalo, now feeds cattle and sheep;
Here is health and wealth and plenty for Dakota land is cheap.
White men now are settled where savages tepees were found;
On thriving farms and ranches, all rich and fertile ground.
Why don't you come to Dakota this land so fair and free;
It's the land that suits the people and it's the land for me.

Yes, we did have droughts some years in the sections away from the river valleys that took in our section of Stark County. The oldest settlers claimed that North Dakota had a bonanza crop every seven years, and in between it was a "hit or miss" with the rain clouds. Vegetation seemed to grow rankly and profusely, even with very little rain, and this was very noticeable on virgin soil and the wild grasses on gumbo lands. As long as the land was not overly cultivated, it could hold the moisture and produce some kind of a crop. The big bonanza crops every few years always jumped North Dakota to second place among wheat-growing states. Kansas held first honors.

Dickinson had a rain-praying preacher at that time in the Methodist church. He would call his congregation together on a Tuesday evening for special prayers for rain, and the Lord answered his prayers. After two meetings, a fine rain would come and drench the land. Then the same minister would hold a special Tuesday evening meeting to thank the Lord. A hearty "thank God" would go up from the lips of both saint and sinner alike because they were truly thankful for rain. Abram said that the minister would always choose Tuesday evening for the rain prayers because on that day the Lord was not so encumbered with the petty prayers of the "poor sinners" who made it a habit to pray on Sunday and Wednesday night prayer meetings.

The *Dickinson Press* was, and is today, the foremost newspaper of Stark County. Every once in a while, some ambitious reformer would start a new paper, usually beginning his first editorial with: "We have come to fill a long-felt want" and ending with "this paper has come to stay."

The *Dickinson Press* had no intentions of reforming anybody, and it always filled everybody's wants. It served as a medium through which the latest and most reliable news and information about North Dakota and its people could be distributed throughout the county and far and wide to other states. It took first place with the Bible in every Stark County home, and whatever you wanted to know about the state and "who's who" in the state was printed on its pages. It also kept its subscribers well informed on worldwide events, and without any "ballyhoo" it gave the facts and figures. Knute said, "It tells you when I's goes to youse house and youse goes to my's house."

Maggie Day taught her children how to read and spell from the *Dickinson Press*. Without a dictionary in the house, she referred to the newspaper whenever a word stumped her; for this reason, she kept a year's issue always on file. When she was asked about a birth or death, she would find the account in one of the "stale" papers.

Max Hunkle was too busy to read the paper through the spring, summer, and fall—or when he was plowing his fields, growing hay, and harvesting—so he packed every copy of the *Dickinson Press* for eight months in a barrel. He would then read them during the months that he was free from working: in the severely cold winter. It was surprising how many things happened in his own community that he didn't know. He found out when he was toasting his feet on the rail of his frump-heater stove in the evenings and delving through his barrel of papers beside him.

His near neighbors seemed to delight in keeping important news away from Max until he read it in the winter evenings. Births, marriages, and deaths came as surprises. He did miss out once, though, when the number on one of his lottery tickets won a genuine American Waltham watch in a Dickinson jewelry store, and the announcement was made in an April edition, but Max did not read about it until December—too late to claim the watch. A press reporter got the story and made this comment, "Watch out, Max, w'at-ch-do without a watch?"

Another Easterner had settled on his 160 acres near Taylor. He got his land under cultivation, brought his family out from Indiana, and was so busy that he had not visited any other town in North Dakota. All he knew about the country he read in the *Dickinson Press*, and he was mightily impressed with the county seat.

He was more than impressed with the editorials in the paper, and on his first visit to Dickinson he made straight for the office of the *Dickinson Press*. No one seemed to be around when he opened the door cautiously, and poking his head in a suggestive sort of way, as if there were more to see, he inquired, "Is this the editorial rinktum?"

A man sitting at a desk looked up and asked, "The what, my friend?"

The Easterner edged himself in a little more and looked around. "Is this the rinktum, sinktum, sanctum, or whatever you call the place where editors live?"

"This is the editorial room, sir; won't you come in please?"

"No, I guess I won't come in! I just wanted to see what a rinktum was like, that's all! This looks like our garret, *[attic]*, only worse! Good day, Mr. Editor!" The Easterner went back to Taylor.

The *Dickinson Press* still carries the news as the home newspaper of Stark County. It never did say, "This paper has come to stay," but it just had to stay because the people could not get along without it. The first editor has passed on, but the spirit of the old *Dickinson Press* has been kept alive by new editors, and now that little paper ranks as foremost in North Dakota, and it carries its message to every state in the Union.

## Covered Wagons

It was not a common sight at that time to see a covered wagon drawn by two horses or mules coming slowly into Taylor on the main road from the East. They were getting fewer and fewer. Sometimes their destination was Stark County; then again, they were bound for a state farther west or even the Pacific Coast.

These wagon trains always aroused a great deal of curiosity in town when they arrived, and everyone was very courteous to the newcomers. Father was always foremost to meet them, and I would hang onto his hand or his coat tail just to get a peek inside of the

## Land Offices and Town Stores

semicylindrical top to see if there were any children or babies or cats and dogs huddled in the wagon bed.

Very often the tired traveler would stop at the hotel for a night to get a hot bath, a good dinner, and a good night's sleep in a real bed. The majority of covered-wagon travelers could not afford this, but if they stopped near the hotel, Mother and Father were sure to visit them and offer them something to add to their comfort.

I have many pleasant memories of friends we made through these chance meetings of the covered-wagon trains. Father said these brave people were the salt of the earth, and they made the best citizens. They had the guts to get out of a rut and find a place that offered them the greatest opportunity to grow progressively. Father made many a coast-bound traveler change his mind and build a farm or ranch on our boundless prairies. He loved the freedom of expansion and in all sincerity showed the possibilities to others.

I recall vividly the morning that a very dilapidated covered wagon arrived in Taylor and stopped in front of the hotel. The two horses even looked too weak and undernourished to go any farther. A young woman came into the office and asked if some woman would look at her baby, since there was no doctor in town. Mother brought the baby in—a little girl of eighteen months. She fed her cereal, cream, and hot milk. This was all the medicine she needed as she went to sleep smiling: no more whimpering or whining for food.

This was Abe and Adell Neuhut and their baby Nellie from Salem, Kansas. Both Abe and Adell were schoolteachers and had lost all they owned in one of those freak tornados that picked out a few farms and scattered everything to the winds. They did not have the heart to start new. Adell had an uncle in Montana who had offered them a good inducement to come out there. It took all their savings to make the trip, and now they were almost at the end of their rope.

One side of their canvas-covered top was decorated with an inscription in large black-charcoal lettering: "I'm for Colorado and irrigation; I'm through with Kansas and starvation; I'm going to my wife's relation and make a good demonstration!"

That night they were invited into the hotel, and Father and the neighbors looked over the traveling outfit. It was a sad sight and not equal to the long journey. Father wanted to make a suggestion to Abe, so he took his own original way. He did some fancy lettering on the other side of the canvas wagon cover: "Why don't you stay in North Dakota, where there is no irrigation? With your good education you can engage in speculation. Bring your own and wife's relation. Here is rich and free salvation; this is worth consideration. It's the truth and has foundation!"

This little rhyme turned the tide for Abe and Adell Neuhut. They filed on 160 acres of level farming land and remained as dependable citizens. Adell cherished that old charcoal-lettered wagon cover, and I presume it is still in the family.

## The Taylor Stores

I like to close my eyes and envision the little town of Taylor, as I knew it in my girlhood, including the long Front Street, where all the big business was transacted. All business seemed to be a public affair and of great interest to everyone, near and far. There was a brotherly love feeling with a "help-thy-neighbor" spirit that enveloped the settlers and placed all others as outsiders. Everyone tried to do business in their hometown, and when anything could not be had there, they gave the dealer of that commodity the order to obtain it elsewhere. There was always a friendly "howdy" from everyone you met, with a sincere inquiry about your family and how you were doing.

Intermarriage between the various groups of settlers of all nationalities was so common that the state was building a strong and hardy stock of people. Tall, rangy, powerful, inclined to leanness were the young men of North Dakota, while it's young women had a wholesome type of strong beauty: useful and practical as well as ornamental. I remember asking Father once if I would be beautiful when I grew up. The question seemed to stun him, and he said, "Ye gods; you'll have to learn, my Dotty, that beauty is more than skin deep!"

The Westerners were very free with their money; so bargains did not appeal to them. All stores had a one price for all with a reasonable amount for profit. Prices had to come out even money. Pennies were not in circulation in the West. You paid five cents, ten cents, twenty-five cents, fifty cents, and one dollar. Change that was made had to be done with those denominations of money. It was a laughing joke when a Westerner went east and was asked for forty-nine cents or ninety-eight cents for an article. He would hand the salesman or saleslady the full silver piece and say, "Keep the change."

James Holcum from Halliday took two carloads of cattle to St. Louis and then stayed two weeks to visit his wife's relatives. The streetcar fare was four cents and eight cents on some lines. James would insist on paying five and ten cents on his rides, while the conductors would stare at him open-mouthed. "Why didn't you take the pennies?" his wife asked when he returned.

"Oh, I couldn't be bothered with all those pennies! Who in hell wants to clutter up the pockets of his chaparajos with such tripe-toting?" His wife figured up that James threw away about nine dollars in pennies when visiting her relatives.

## Drug Store

The most attractive and sales-appealing store on Front Street was the Taylor Drug Store, and it was a "store of all wares," even more so than the present-day drug store. Carl Deming, the proprietor, was not a pharmacist or a chemist, and he did not need to be as he sold everything out of a bottle or package. No matter what ailed you, he had a cure.

Dagget Hunt was his very efficient and energetic clerk. Dag went in very strong for window advertising. He would whittle a cake of soap to a point, and with much flourishing in fancy lettering he would print a new advertisement every Saturday morning on the large front windows of the store. This attracted the weekend trade and boosted sales. I shall never forget those window ads. Maple and I would spell out the words and even try to imitate the big flourish to the capital letters.

Once a window blazed: "If you want to dye pretty and be happy, come in and buy a bottle of Leaman's Dye Colors. If you don't want to dye, try our Dry Kalsomine." Another ad read: "Don't be seen out on the street with freckles, tan, or moth patches. You don't have to buy our White Rose Glycerin! If you can afford it, we will give you a bottle free!"

This ad filled two windows:

> Take home an arm full of things for 1 Dollar; 1 Pound of Coffee, with a chance in the Lottery on a hand-carved, eight-day Clock, 1 Pound of Lily Starch, 3 bars of American Bleacher soap, 1 Bottle each of Dr. Price's Vanilla Extract and Lemon Extract, 1 Box Cragin's Stove Polish, 1 Box Hotchkiss Shoe Blacking. You can also exchange for anything else you prefer.

This advertisement brought in the ranchers and farmers: "Save your horses and cattle, ask for some Assafoedite. Ask for a cooling Soda to quiet your own nerves. No Soda Water sold on Sundays."

Dagget Hunt liked to write such advertisements as this to keep things moving: "We have any kind of Oil you want: Kerosene, Machine, Neat's foot, Safety Anchor, Linseed, Castor, and Olive."

## Land Offices and Town Stores

Here is another I remember: "We sell pocketbooks, music, and Hotchkiss Lozenges." On the other window was "Full Scholarship in Bismarck Business College for sale cheap by the Druggist."

Carl Demming kept drugs and all kinds of patent medicines for any ailment of man or beast. His greatest seller, and good-for-all-ills medicine, was Hops Bitters *[made from herbs]*, which made a man of seventy-eight feel like a man of thirty. The fact that North Dakota was a prohibition state made this quite a necessity to one who needed a quick pick-up for his or her nervous system. One of Daggett's best window ads took the two front panes: "The first object of the American people is to 'get rich'; the second, how to regain good health. The first can be obtained by energy, honesty, and saving; the second, by using Green's August Flower."

Doctor Stickney in Dickinson was our nearest doctor, and he would stop at the Taylor Drug Store when in the locality and fill his own prescriptions. He would always stop at our hotel if he were in Taylor any length of time. Doctor had the right idea about sickness—far in advance of many doctors at that time: he believed in giving nature a chance to heal and cure without any hindrance of drugs.

Sometimes he would go into mother's pantry and get the powdered sugar can, and Maple and I would watch him folding this harmless mixture in little papers, making a very professional "powder" for a neurotic patient.

Sometimes he would leave a goblet of sweetened water at a bedside with instructions for the patient to take a teaspoonful every few hours until well. This good medicine had the right psychological effect to bring about a cure—with none of the evil effects of drugs—for this type of patient. Doctor Stickney explained to us as we watched him: "The majority of people want to take medicine for every little ill. If I didn't give them medicine, they would lose faith in me, so I give them this, even when it is all in their mind. It is good, and because they believe in me, they are cured!"

## General Store

The Taylor General Store had the congenial atmosphere of a men's country club. The townsmen would gather there to meet the farmers and ranchers when they came in to do their trading. It seemed to be the ideal place to gossip, swap yarns, and tell long stories about their respective countries or states.

The proprietor was Lewis Lewiston, a stalwart, bony-framed Norwegian, who was an easygoing man and who welcomed his customers and even the "stickers-on" who never spent five cents in his store. Lewis was slow in waiting on his customers, and it was just too bad if anyone was in a hurry. He would measure off calico by the yard, then hold a jug under the dripping molasses barrel, then weigh out a handful of crackers, and perhaps next measure hemp or jute rope.

No one thought about sanitary conditions then. All foodstuffs came in bulk, barrels, and boxes, and hands and fingers seemed to be in everything, with no thought of germs.

The store was a long frame building with an open porch in front, and it had large show windows, which were well stocked with the contents of the store, with no show of window decorations. If something new came in, the box or barrel sat in the window. A bright bolt of gingham or calico would be displayed, and a suit of men's blue denim overalls would swing on a hanger. Cowboy outfits always seemed in great demand: plaid shirts in gay combinations, with sheep-lined snaps, or long-fringed cowhide chaparajos.

On one side of the store, as you entered, were the yard goods and notions, some men's and women's apparel, and also clothing for children and babies. On the left-hand side were the groceries of all kinds: canned goods and glass jars on the shelves, and in front of the counters were barrels of vinegar, molasses, kerosene, crackers, and cookies.

The back of the store seemed to be packed from floor to ceiling with about everything that was needed inside and outside of a

## Land Offices and Town Stores

home. Lewis had a perfect memory for his store commodities and where he kept them. If he was asked for anything that was not in sight, he would dive in the midst of things, entirely disappear, and then come out with the article in his hand. If he did not have what you wanted, he would humbly apologize, and he would have it the next time you called.

Lewis had to carry the accounts of most of the farmers and ranchers on his books. Most of them were dependable. The farmer received his bog income every fall after threshing and would then pay up all his debts and start a clean slate. The rancher had an income twice a year: selling stock for market and culling out his herd. All Western business seemed to be on charge accounts of six months or a year, and dealers were prepared for this.

I remember one time when Lewis had a few bad accounts that were not paid when sales were made, so Dagget Hunt came to his assistance with his flourishing soap pencil on the General Store window. It read: "We heard you made a sale! How about coming in and settling that little bill you owe! We are not made of money in here like a banker—or an editor!"

It was amusing to watch May from the south side do her trading. She would say to Lewis, "I want some first-class dried apricots."

He would ask in his slow drawl, "How many pounds do you want, May?" and he would open the large box on the counter.

May would say, "Why, I want the whole box, of course! We eat at our ranch!"

Then Lewis would start measuring out about five pounds and close the box. "This is all I'll let you have today, May. Have to keep the rest for my other customers." Then she would ask for some "writin' paper envelopes" and demand the whole box—one great gross. "Oh, go on, May, you'll never write that many letters in your whole life," and Lewis would count out for her twenty-four envelopes. Sometimes he would not ask her how much she wanted of anything, and then he would give her what he thought was sufficient and mark it down in the book. "May would buy my whole store if I'd let her," he would say.

Once Albert Anderson walked in the store from the "3 A" ranch and said, "My wife is going east this summer with little Albert; she's goin' to Asbury Park in New Jersey. Do you suppose you can order a bathing suit for Albert? He's six years old!"

"Yes, I can order it, but why spend the money? From what I hear, boys of that age only wear a wad of cotton in each ear. You can also tie a red yarn string around his neck to hold the key to his clothes bag. And that's the way I used to go bathing!" and Lewis went on measuring out the flannel.

"That would suit me all right, but the wife wants a real bathing suit," said Albert, "and what my wife says goes! You know my wife!" Then Lewis drawled out, "Well, to tell the truth, I don't even know what a boy's bathing suit looks like, let alone selling them."

Maple and I liked to go in all the stores with Father. His personality filled the place. He would chat and laugh with the storekeeper and always order more things than Mother had on her list. He would always tell us to look things over and see if there was anything we wanted, and what we wanted, we got. We were both practical in our wants. When in the General Store, Maple would pick out overshoes, a pencil box, or a dish for the cats. I would pick out the brightest bolt of calico and have Lewis measure off one-fourth yard or look through the notions for something that I could use playing "doll dressmaker."

We would both look longingly in the candy case and note all the different kinds: butterscotch squares, licorice root sticks, red and white candy sticks, chocolate creams and peppermint sticks, and coconut cakes and caramels. We denied ourselves candy because the traveling dentist who stopped at the hotel twice a year told us not to eat too much sweets in candy or sugar or it would spoil our strong white teeth and take the roses out of our cheeks.

Occasionally, Father would treat us to candy, but he admired the willpower we showed that was backed by pride and the eternal feminine way.

## Taylor Shoe Store

Taylor could boast of a shoemaker who considered his trade an art. He made shoes to order, and only one grade, the best, out of genuine leather. He would give a guarantee with every pair; that is, he said, "I guarantee them for life—if you don't live too long." He also said of his repair work, "When I repair other makes of shoes, I put a salesman out of business."

Harvey was a man with a past, but no one had ever heard the truth about the first chapters of his life. He had drifted out west and no one knew which state he hailed from. He had traveled a great deal and had lived in many states in the East and South. He had the accent of both places. Harvey had an education above the average and some degree of culture, but he tried to hide it behind a rough, pretended exterior manner. One could understand Harve's dual personality when they knew that he was a periodic drunkard and would drink anything alcoholic from rotgut whiskey to lemon extract and all other bitters that were sold as tonics either for men or women.

When Harve was sober, he was a quiet, retiring man with a gracious personality, who lived in his book-filled shack and was sufficient unto himself for company and entertainment. He was friendly toward all but leaned toward those with higher intelligence who could talk above the commonplace things of life. Father was one of his best friends, but even he could not pierce his shell. The "cobbler" owned one of the neatest little shack-houses on Main Street: a gay-looking building painted white with red trim and the only place that could boast of a sidewalk in front of the lot. This was his shoemaking shop and his home. Over the door was a sign: "Boots and Shoes, Custom-made work; Eastern in all its variety, from a fine calf boot to a metallic-toed shoe. Repairing sewed and pegged. Hard Pan Prices."

There was a large bay window in front of the shop where Harve sat at his shoemaker's bench when he was on the job. When the sign was down, everyone knew that he was in the back bedroom of his home fighting elephants and rattlesnakes and those little imps of Satan who perched on his bedposts to taunt him with jeers or mock at his helplessness and weakness. When Harve was in this delirium (fighting the demons that were possessing his soul and body), Father would stay with him for hours, forcing him to take milk and broths and gradually soothing him back to normalcy. It was during these periods that Harve would talk about Mary. He would call to her, plead with her to come back to him, and break down and cry and implore her to forgive him for what he was and for all his shortcomings.

Mary seemed to have been the one and only woman in his life—the one and only thing that he cared for or loved. Nothing else mattered but Mary, and the pitiful way he would call her name with the long drawn-out sound of the vowel, "Ma-a-a-ry," brought tears to the eyes of those who heard. Then he would caress the name lovingly and endearingly, "Ma-a-a-ry, darling!" and "Ma-a-a-ry, life of my life!" "Sun of my soul!" and when he would quiet down to sleep from exhaustion, he would breathe the name "Ma-a-a-ry" until he would wake up sober.

Abram asked him about Mary and said, "Why don't you send for Mary to come here, Harve? If you love a woman like that you would have the willpower to keep sober with her beside you!" But Harve never sent for Mary or knew if Mary was alive. No one ever knew, but Harve cherished and lived for this secret love, and as time went on, everyone in and around Taylor knew the story. Those who loved to gossip found this savory at all times to spur on the imagination.

My memory loves to linger over those unforgettable characters of my childhood. Every person in that little pioneer town of Taylor made a lasting impression. My world was so small: its interests seemed bounded by the state line of North Dakota, and then in the far distance was the state of New Jersey, where we migrated. Outside of that, the whole world was as far away as the planet Mars, and all was just as vague.

## Blacksmith and Whitesmith Shop

There was another building on Main Street that was more interesting to Maple and me than a museum would have been. It was the blacksmith shop of Samuel Buel, a long, low shed-like building that seemed cluttered up with machinery, and there was room for horses to be brought in to be shod. In back of this was a three-room apartment—bedroom, living room, and kitchen—that Sam called home.

Over the shed was a sign: "Sam Buel, Blacksmith! Horse Nails, hammered and pressed. Nail Rods, Anvils, Vices, Drills. A Complete Stock of Blacksmith's Goods and Tools." On the other side was another sign: "We mend everything, even a Broken Boozer!"

Sam certainly believed in signs as there was another sign near the door: "Blacksmith and Whitesmith." This name was most intriguing, as we never saw him doing any whitesmithing. He said that he could mend white things like tin or silver, and one day I took one of mother's large cooking kettles in to be mended. It had a large hole in the bottom. Mother had brought this kettle from New Jersey, and it was such a nice kettle that our kitchen would be lost without it. It was one of Mother's wedding presents.

Sam looked at it and then melted a big piece of solder that covered the hole and seemed to round out the whole bottom. The kettle just rocked after that, and when it sat on a hot stove with the contents boiling, it rocked back and forth in a stupid rhythm. When Maple and I would come in the kitchen and the kettle was boiling and rocking, we would sing: "Rockabye, Baby," and then I composed new words to fit the rocking kettle.

> "Rockabye, Kettle, on the stove top.
> When the fire burns, the kettle will rock;
> When the solder breaks, the kettle will fall
> Over the head of Sam Buel, that's all!"

This song lasted through our childhood, but the kettle lasted longer. I would wager a bet that it is still in service: boiling and rocking in perfect rhythm in the kitchen of a farmhouse northeast of Taylor because that is where I heard of it at a very late date.

Besides being a blacksmith and a whitesmith, Sam was a hunter of wild animals. The latter part of November (when business would become rather dull), Sam would turn the keys in the locks of both doors, call his malamute dog, Heliva, and hire himself to the Badlands or the borderline of Canada to hunt for the rest of the winter.

He would drive his two faithful horses, Pro and Con, hitched to a large lumber wagon with a double box. He would carry everything that he needed—sleeping bag and plenty of grub—and would join other hunters and trappers in that vast, frozen, snow-laden country.

Sam had a big kind heart and loved animals and would often let an animal go free if he could not get it in a humane way. He would not hunt with cruel traps, which usually catch an animal by a paw or else crush its back and hold it for hours in cruel torture. Sam was a crack shot with a rifle and could land his game with one bullet in the right place. He did all he could to keep other hunters from committing outrageous atrocities on defenseless fur-bearing animals.

Some hunters would hunt and trap every animal that crossed their path unless, by their prowess, they proved too shrewd and wary. Sam hunted only for good pelts with a density of fur and long over hair, which is the beauty and pride of a fur garment and marks its chief value with the furrier. This Dakota huntsman would not kill an animal that was suckling its young, but often heartbreaking things would happen, and Sam would come home with an animal baby to raise and add to his pets.

That was one reason Maple and I liked to visit Sam's blacksmith shop. He could pet his horses and Heliva, and sometimes there would be an antelope, a coyote, a badger, or a muskrat. The badger and muskrat dug under his house and undermined it. He reinforced it just in time to keep it from collapsing. He had a way with animals so that they did not fear him, and he could not kill one that trusted him. The latter part of March, Sam would come back, his wagon filled to an overload with the finest furs—soft, silky, and downy.

Abram was the local agent for furs. They were put in the large storehouse adjoining the kitchen. Furs were tacked on the walls and rafters and hung from beams. Sometimes the room would be completely filled with furs when Matthias would arrive from St. Paul to buy them.

Even now I can see how he looked when Matthias examined the pelts. He would feel the texture, stroke and pull the hair filaments, and praise or swear at each pelt as he sorted them out for their intrinsic value. He would take two of Sam's beaver pelts—soft rich fur with a golden blend—and he would make a roll of one and cross it around his neck and with the other make a rounded muff for his hands. Then he would strut into the kitchen with a dainty mincing walk so that Mother and the girls could see him.

"Take a look at this, Mrs. Berry! This will strike the eye of some millionaire's wife in New York or Paris. It can vie *[compete]* with her precious gems and jewels, or the Great Kahn of Tartary might buy enough of these glorious pelts to make a court coat! Now wait, I'll show you the difference in furs!"

He would take two of the mild-weather, straggly haired pelts and make a silly looking neckpiece and an equally ridiculous-looking muff. Then he would strike a pose like a bowery dancer: his arms akimbo, his rear end elevated, and his neck sticking out like a gamecock. Thus he would stride through the kitchen and ask, "Don't this mangy fur set look like hell bent for auction?"

Maple and I loved the show he would put on and would hand him more fur pelts to pose in. We knew the good furs from the bad, and he knew that the conditions of food and weather were responsible for the difference. Matthias used to say, "It's just the same with man as with beast: with favorable conditions he can raise a good head of glossy hair on his ivory dome, or he can have a dull, straggly thatch like this poor, climate-bound, eat-what-he-can-find muskrat! I tell you, good hair depends on inside and outside condition, and maybe someday we'll learn how to regulate these things. Gray hair is starved hair! Look at this badger!" And he'd hold up a scattered-haired pelt that looked like seaweed.

Matthias liked to compare his own head of thick, glossy-brown hair to the perfect midwinter pelts of lustrous furs. When young men would ask him for the secret of his healthy hair, he would only say, "Right living, young man, right living!" They walked away and pronounced him "half loco." Besides being a blacksmith, whitesmith, and hunter, Sam Buel was an inventor. He invented most of the gadgets used around his shop. His bellows worked automatically with less pumping because he had a contraption attached, which he said was "almost perpetual motion." He made his own horseshoes—broadly U-shaped so they were kind to horses' feet and made them sure footed on the rough prairie turf.

He invented a swinging trap door at the bottom of his exit door that his cats could operate and go and come without leaving the door open for prairie gophers or field mice to find their way in. He also invented a sugar bowl that would measure off one spoonful of sugar at a time. He sent many of his inventions to Washington and had them patented, but that was all Sam ever did about them.

Sam liked children, and when they would ask questions, he would never answer, "Oh, that's to make little boys and girls ask questions!" He never insulted a child's intelligence. He would answer every question and even stop work to demonstrate or explain. When I asked him, "Sam, why does a screw, screw?" he showed me the different kinds of screws: lag screw, wood screw, saw screw, cap screw and skein screw. He explained how each was grooved in an advancing spiral on its surface, then he would turn it slowly. "See how it cuts its way in! Why, a screw just can't help but screw!"

## Berry Family Scrapbook and Diary

Father had two praiseworthy hobbies: a scrapbook and a diary, for which I now bless him and thank him from the bottom of my heart. The scrapbook was started way back in 1836 by several of Father's very sentimental and poetry-loving ancestors. It has been added to along the years, and then Grandma Berry in Chester, New Jersey, preserved many clippings of the Civil War, political controversies, and the poetry of that era. When Grandma was sure that Abram was going to make his home in North Dakota, she sent the precious old scrapbook to him, packed carefully in a box with bolts of flannel and all-wool material, mittens, wool stockings, and a lot of useful little gadgets for Mother to use in the house. Those surprise boxes would come to us about every three months. Maple and I took them for granted then, but when I grew up, I appreciated all the love and devotion that dear thoughtful Grandma packed in those boxes and the unspeakable joy they gave us in our prairie home.

Abram delighted in going on with the scrapbook with clippings from our western pipers, personal clippings of his business transactions, and the social affairs of Taylor. The news in the *Dickinson Press* was local, and nothing escaped those reporters with their "nose for news." His diary was carefully written: a synopsis of our western life, amusing incidents, and all the important things that happened. He found his diary very helpful in referring to it when any argument came up. He claimed that he had won two lawsuits in court by keeping a dated, fact-giving diary of his business transactions, and this had been sufficient proof to save him thousands of dollars.

His father, Joseph B. Berry, and his mother, Mary Melick Berry, were proud of their son and shared his accomplishments through the scrapbook. They wrote, "Abram was a justice of the peace, fur buyer, Indian trader, grain elevator agent, grain grower, rancher, and sheep raiser." He became a veterinarian, and armed with a veterinary book and instruments obtained from a mail order house, he was ready to doctor sick animals.

*Chapter Three -*
# The Sioux State

Abram loved North Dakota, the state he had chosen for his home. He liked to "spout" all the facts he knew about the "Sioux state" to Easterners and the transient guests who stopped at the hotel. He would boast that North Dakota was famous for this and for that. "North Dakota has an area of 70,637 square miles of land that is richer and more productive than the valley of the Nile," he would say. "North Dakota has one hour more sunshine every day of its growing season than any other area of the United States because its horizon line is not shaded by mountains." Then he would proudly tell his listeners, "The wild 'prairie rose' is our state flower, and no cultivated rose can surpass it in beauty and fragrance!"

Another claim for his state was: "The western meadowlark is voted officially our bird, and this is the grand opera singer of all birds!" The climax of all his boasts was this: "The motto of our 'Sioux state' is 'Liberty and Union, Now and Forever, One and Inseparable,' and when I add that we are all live Republicans, it means that North Dakota is not a state divided against itself!"

I recall the time that Dermott Twining, a lawyer from Pierre, South Dakota, was staying at the hotel and started a heated argument with Father by saying that South Dakota was admitted to the Union before North Dakota. They argued and argued, but neither could prove his point, so Father wrote to the District of Columbia for the actual facts. Even the annals of Washington, DC, could not prove which of the twin states was admitted to the Union first. It seems that President Harrison signed both documents admitting both North and South Dakota to the Union, but each paper was exactly alike, covered completely with wording, except for the space for the signature, so there was no way to tell which document the president signed first.

Abram stuck to his point that North Dakota was the oldest of the twin states because, naturally, one always speaks of North and South Dakota, and the papers would lay side by side in that order for signing. Dermott Twining gave in at best just before leaving the hotel. He paid Father one dollar, the amount he bet, and stood treat for the house. Father called everybody in, and they clicked glasses with whiskey, beer, and ginger ale, proving for all time that North Dakota was the oldest of the twin states.

His diary told him that the name "Dakota" had a deeper meaning than the white man understood. He learned this from a Sioux Indian Chief. *Dakota*, translated in the Sioux language, means "allies," but the deeper Indian interpretation means "very close, intermixed like a blood brother." That is a very close bond in the Indian tribes. North Dakota was the home of the Sioux Indians, and they were the only Indians we knew. The government reservation was not very far away from us, so we saw the Indians often and got to know some of them very well. It is said that the Indian is like the elephant: "he never forgets." Anyway, it is true that the Indians we knew did not have faith and trust in a white person unless he or she had proven his or her honesty and sincerity.

Abram won their confidence and trust from the very first time he laid eyes on an Indian. They singled him out as the one and only white man in Taylor whom they wanted to do business with. They gave him a long Indian name, which I cannot remember, but, translated, it meant "Big Man Who Laughs." They could not find a name more appropriate, and as Lyman Cary from Mandan said, "It shows that the Indian has a fine, subtle sense of humor." Lyman stayed at the hotel for months at a time, selling real estate (town lots and farms) and also insurance to cover life and property. He said that Father had the agency for about everything that was bought and sold on the "fly" and about the biggest "flying business" he ever saw one man handle.

Father was agent for the Mandan Roller Mills Company and bought No. #1 hard wheat and oats, durum wheat, rye, and flaxseed from the Stark County farmers. They had erected a barge warehouse on the north side of the railroad tracks, with a side track leading to it, where the freight cars were loaded with those plump, yellow kernels of wheat.

I heard Lyman Gary say: "Our North Dakota wheat kernels are so large that when an Easterner first casts his eyes on them, he thinks they are a new kind of bean." Such was the wheat that was raised on the sun-kissed prairies, aided by an extra hour of sunshine every day. They had that extra flavor, and they had vitamins plus and double-plus, but science had not yet discovered them. The office in the large warehouse was the main office where Father transacted all of his "flying business." The north side of the building was off from Front Street with a road leading to the ground-level Fairbanks's Scales, where the wagons and their loads were weighed.

Father's office was fitted out complete with office furniture ordered from Montgomery Ward and Company's catalog: a large roll-top desk, swivel-seat chair, the largest filing cabinet they sold, a table and several extra chairs, a fire- and bullet-proof safe, and a high-swung typewriter. He said that he held every office in his "flying businesses": he was president, vice-president, treasurer, and secretary of every one, and his salary was what was left after everything else was paid.

Father had a very foresighted wisdom, which held him in good faith with his neighbors without giving them information about his personal affairs. Maple and I were often questioned by the most inquisitive, and our answers would be Father's exact word, which would often be too ridiculous to be funny or too silly to be simple. Once a nosy body asked me: "Does your father charge all those men who hang around the hotel to eat?"

I was so glad to inform her, "Oh no, Papakins has adopted some of those men, and he never charges those he adopts. He is always adopting somebody."

Father's business with the Indians was quite apart from all else. He called it his American business, and he would tell everyone, "Here is where I am dealing with: the true American, the American Indian!"

## Sioux Indians

A caravan of Sioux Indians would come into Taylor from the reservation about twice a year with their large lumber wagons loaded with pea beans or bleached bones from the prairies. The Indian braves would bring their squaws and papooses with them, and pack ponies would follow the wagons with their camping paraphernalia, the painted animal hides for their teepees, and the teepee poles dragging each side of the ponies. They would come well prepared to stay several weeks, and an interpreter would come with them to see that they were honestly dealt with.

The interpreter we all liked the best was Juttan, a half-breed Indian who was educated in an Eastern school and who proved an equal combination of white man and Indian. Sometimes he would express himself in well-spoken English, and then again he would shrug his shoulders and give the typical Indian grunt. He never learned how to laugh; he made the attempt when Father cracked a joke that he could understand, and then be would open his mouth wide and make a noise like our laughter, but the muscles of his face would not change expression. In fact, it would belie *[disguise]* his mirth. It was our delight to try to make Juttan laugh.

When the Indians arrived in Taylor, they would ask for "Big Man Who Laughs" and positively refuse to do business with anyone else. They would drive to the warehouse, and as each load was driven on the scales and weighed, Berry would stand at the door and tally it and credit it to the Indian's name. He would pay them in silver and count out the silver dollars in their dirty red palms. They would grunt their thanks and then unload their bones on the ground near the side tracks. The peas were put in large gunnysacks and sold to the town merchants.

Maple and I were always amused to see Father's Indian bookkeeping, using the Indian name with the amount of the transaction: "Running-Buck, No-Feather, Wolf-in-Hole, White Tomahawk, Jumping Badger, Big Foot, Lone Bull, Crazy Horse, Crooked Toe, and Comes Walking." There were many others that I cannot remember. In later years, a very unkind souvenir collector stole the Indian ledger from Father's desk.

The Indians found the dried, bleached bones on the prairies—the bones of wild and tame animals that had died on the plains. The bones could be found in the tall grasses or sometimes partly buried in the gumbo bogs and ravines and gullies or in the bottom of the dry riverbeds. Sometimes human bones would be found among them: the skull of a white man or Indian and other parts of the human anatomy. We would always look the bone piles over carefully to take out all the human bones before they were shipped to a St. Louis Sugar Refinery Company. There the bones were made into an animal charcoal, which was used in the process of sugar manufacturing. Some were sold to a fertilizer company.

The human skulls and crossbones were sent to medical schools, or sometimes a guest at the hotel would buy a set to make an ornament for his or her study or den. One cannot account for the morbid tendencies of some very refined men and women. Human bones were in great demand.

I remember when Judge Morcum of Calumet, Michigan, stopped at the hotel one week, trying to make a land deal with Lyman Gary. He found a well-preserved Indian skull with all the good teeth intact and two thighbones that were not too weathered. He spent all his spare time in his room sandpapering and polishing those bones and then mounting them on a slab of Badlands quartzite, with its zigzag lines of white, pink, purple, and brown minerals. This took on a high polish, and with the grinning skull staring at you with sightless eyes, you felt cold shivers running up and down your spine as you looked at the gruesome ornament.

When these large caravans of Indian traders arrived in Taylor, it was just as if a circus had come to town. The news would spread far into the country, and farmers and ranchers would bring their families in to see the Indians. Some brought in produce to make trades with them.

After the Indians had unloaded their bones and pea beans, they would drive to the northern outskirts of Taylor and make their camp. They would surround it with their wagons in a semicircle and with their ponies hobbled or tethered outside to feed on the prairie grass. The squaws would do all the work in camp while the braves wrapped their blankets around themselves and squatted leisurely before the fire. They were the "braves" and absolutely free from any occupation or menial work.

The Indian squaws would go about their work in a slow methodical way, and by their expressionless faces, one could not fathom their thoughts or even know if they were pleased or unhappy with their work. They would usually come to town dressed in their own original garments: animal skins made soft and pliable, embroidered with beads and straws or elaborately painted with strange designs. Many squaws had a papoose fastened very securely in a sort of pocket on their backs and held by a belt or wampum.

The weight of the child did not hinder the squaws' movements when about their camp duties. The poor little things would bob up and down as their mothers erected the tent poles and wrapped the animal skins around them. The teepees seemed very easy to adjust after they were unrolled. The long piles were secured in the ground and the flap poles made an overlapping door with two ears sticking out above. I suppose that this was the Indian's

## The Sioux State

idea for ventilation. Then there were pins, which held the flap doors tighter securely, and pegs were used at the bottom to hold the tent covering close to the ground. These comical tents were very picturesque, with gay paintings on the animal skins, which were smooth and well-tanned. The paintings were of both wild and tame animals and Indians in crude drawings, and each told a story of some outstanding bravery in their lives. Juttan would tell us these stories, and through him we learned a great many things about Indian life: their habits, their traditions, and a peek into the hidden recesses of their character.

Abram had a great understanding and sympathy for Indians. He felt that the early white people who drove them from their lands with deadly gunfire had treated them so unjustly. He said, "Our early American history is nothing to be proud of. In fact, the way our ancestors dealt with the Indians makes me ashamed to be classed as one of their descendants." I have heard Father preach this many a time and then add this phrase; "The so-called 'civilized people' came to America after Columbus discovered it, with a Bible in one hand and a whiskey bottle in the other hand! They degraded the land and deprived the Indian tribes of their God-given freedom and then pronounced the Indians a savage race!"

Juttan had enough white blood in his veins to make him feel that he was one of us, and his Indian blood held him to the Indians to help and aid them all that was possible. It was from Juttan that Father got his insight of the inner feelings and the lonely heart longings of these subdued Indians who were forced to live according to white men's whims and white men's dictation on the vary land that had once been their own.

The policy of the United States was to place all the tribes on reservations and prohibit them from wandering and also to prohibit the white people to live upon this reserved land. In return for this land ceded by them to the United States, the Indians received yearly grants, which were paid in the form of supplies of food, clothing, farm tools, and other necessities. Under these conditions Uncle Sam was attempting to civilize them or change them to our mode of life entirely. It was not easy to change the Indian, and when the stimulus of a self-supporting way of life was wanted, then it was not surprising that slow advance was made.

The Sioux Indians, as we knew them, were a subdued race, living quietly on the reservation, tilling their lands, raising cattle, and ponies and trying to hold on to their religion, which, Father said, was "too beautiful to spoil." While Juttan was educated in our schools and also attended a Sunday school during his childhood, he still clung closely to the Indian religion. Berry learned a great deal from him in little talks when he would come in his offices—in the hotel or at the warehouse.

"The sun is our god, our great father," said Juttan. "He sends warmth and nourishment for us and our animals. The great father loves us and takes care of us always. We are his children. What have you that is greater than the sun?" Juttan would look up at the heavens in great reverence, and when the sun was shining upon him, it was God's, the great father's, nearness, and the moon and stars by night were assuring him and all humankind of care and protection.

Abram would answer, "No, Juttan, we have nothing greater to offer you. Your great father is the sun, and as you believe in him, he will answer you. It is a great conception of God. Hold fast to your god, Juttan, He is the god of the red man and also the god of the white man—the great father!" Abram said that the Indian religion was entirely astrological, and while it was based on sun worship, it brought a realism of God in their consciousness. It is all we can ask of any religion. Our religion can only be what we make it by our thoughts and actions. The Jerseyites liked to tease Father about his Indian clientele, and while the Indians were in town, everyone called him "Big Man Who Laughs."

I overheard this conversation when they were congregated in the hotel office, smoking and chatting. Father was telling Lyman Cary, Ed Harvey, Hamp Stevens, and several others: "The red man has a beautiful and logical religion. Why, this half-educated Juttan is a better philosopher than many of the ethnologists who are still seeking for new cults, not satisfied with their conception of God."

Then one of them said: "They had better call you "big chief who preaches."

But Father went right on talking: "It's a damn fine religion, boys, and a damn good religion! The red man centralized his god in the sun, and he recognized the beneficial influence of all the heavenly bodies that shone alike on all mankind!"

"Yes," said Lyman Gary, "they also bow with reverence to the powers of the four elements: wind, fire, water, and earth. What do you say to that?"

"I can only say," Father answered, "that if I ask each one of you where God is, you would each give me a different answer; the fact is: none of you know. We centralize God in a heaven way up above the clouds. He is ruling the worlds from a golden throne, with winged angels around him, playing continually on golden harps! This is what they tried to teach me in Sunday school in Chester, New Jersey, and then told my mother to keep me home after I was ten years of age. I was blasphemous! I preferred to think up a heaven of my own about then."

I can remember how they all laughed and how I strained my ears to catch every word that Father uttered. "Yes, I stayed out of Sunday school after that. I didn't think much of their heaven or their hell; in fact, the people they sent to hell were often far superior to the poor devils they sent to heaven, superior with innate good. I can't understand why they make so much fuss about the hereafter, while we have got the *now* to live in, and we're either making a heaven or hell out of it right here! God is the power, and if the red man centralizes God in the sun, I guess that gives him power! We can centralize God as absolutely *all*, but a harp-playing heaven doesn't appeal to me. I much prefer a 'happy hunting ground!'"

Then and there, for that phase of my childhood, I had a god that was tangible and real, a real awakening of a power within myself. I had an understanding of a god who was to the entire world what my father was to me. This gave me a very warm understanding of Indians because, through the Indians' god, I found myself and began to think.

While the Indians were camped in Taylor, they took up everyone's time and attention. The Taylorites would visit the Indian camp and watch their habits and mode of life. In the evenings they would be home: the braves squatted around the fire smoking and the squaws preparing the evening meal and always moving about, apparently working at their home duties, but on the surface, nothing seemed to be accomplished.

The sun-dried meat that they cooked in a big pot hung on poles over a wood fire often gave off very appetizing odors; then again, the smell would be different from our taste and sometimes repugnant, so we would make our friendly visit short. The Indians did not exert themselves to welcome their visitors: the braves who were squatted before the fire did not seem to look up but refilled their pipes with black tobacco—black as "sooty Acheron," Father expressed it and puffed away with a few contented grunts. When a person said "How!" to them in greeting, they would answer with a guttural "How!" and go on smoking.

Father got the most grunts out of them and sometimes a word or two, which he knew because he would call each one by name, shake hands with them, and attempt a conversation with staccato English and Indian words. He always visited them with Juttan, who could talk to them. He would urge them to raise bigger crops and come back and tell them to explore the prairies so that there was not a bone left. We would always carry gifts with us: a loaf of bread, cookies and crackers, and hard candy for the papooses. Gifts pleased them; they did not like people who just came to stare, and they were masters at giving these curiosity seekers the "cold shoulder."

During the day, the squaws, with papooses on their backs and some trailing along, would visit the houses in Taylor to watch the "white squaws" do their housework. When Mother and the girls were busy in the kitchen, they would suddenly notice that the room had darkened, and, behold, every window would be filled with peeping Indian squaws, their faces pressed flat against the window panes and the palms of their hands extended on each side of their face. Filling in the gaps would be the papooses of all ages, and the way they were dressed, one could not tell their gender. The little bundled papooses on their backs did not get a fair deal. They could not look in the windows, but they did not complain—not so much by a grunt or a sigh. They just hung there, staring into space. So that is where patience is taught. The Indian is always patient. Time is not a factor in his or her life.

Just what the squaws thought of our mode of work could not be told except by the expressions on their faces; they were perfectly blank, stoically impassive. Maple and I would attempt to entertain them by doing gymnastic antics—somersaults, handsprings, and silly dancing—but our audience would remain unmoved, their eyes taking in everything that went on in the room. Mother would always fill a bag with some eatables and let Maple or I give it to them, but this would not terminate their visit. They would stand there for hours and hours and then slowly move on to another house.

Juttan brought a little Indian girl in to visit us. She was about eight years old and had a pretty name, which, translated, meant "prairie flower." Mother gave us enough of our cast-off clothing to dress her completely. We had her put on woolen underwear, long stockings, petticoats, and a bright red dress. We tied her black braids with red ribbons, but through it all she remained perfectly statuesque, with no expression of pleasure or displeasure. She trotted on back to the camp with Juttan. The next time we saw her she had on her Indian garb: one straight slip, hanging from her shoulders, of beaded buckskin.

Maple and I asked Juttan to give us Indian names. He put his hand on Maple's head of straight, dark-brown shining hair and said, "Fine hay, I call you 'Night Cloud.'" And he picked up my red-gold braids, then looked straight in my face, and said, "I call you what I see: 'Little Eyes Who See Much.'"

I had hoped for a more poetic name, but there was no sentiment in Juttan, and then Father added to this: "I call you what I see, 'Little Nose in Everything.'" These names were often used for us and caused a lot of laughter and merriment.

One of Father's "Indian clients" gave the Taylorites a great deal of amusement. This was "Creeping Kate," a Sioux squaw and widow of a white man who lived at the extreme northern end of the reservation. This was the name she was known by, but it was not known if it was her true Indian name or if it had been saddled on her by a "white brother." The name fit her perfectly as her short legs waddled along under her long skirts; it gave her a creeping walk like a land turtle.

Creeping Kate had been married to a cattle rustler who was accidentally shot when caught branding stray steers. It was proven that Kate had been in with him in his cattle-rustling tricks, but somehow the law overlooked her thievery and let her go free. Creeping Kate was overly honest after that: she would not trust Indian or white man and hardly trusted herself. She would come to Taylor with a caravan of her own wagons loaded with cattle hides—each with her own brand, 0-Bar-K, on the right shoulder.

Kate had her own family working for her: cousins and brothers and a whole raft of her own half-breed children. She looked after her business transactions and gave orders and dominated everyone with her, like a ruling female chief. She had tried very hard to get away from the Indian way of living when she had married Pete Hadrickson and had gone to live in a lumber house on his claim. Pete bought everything from mail-order houses, necessities, luxuries, and more than they could ever use. He thought he was a rich man; rustling was so easy: just put his brand on a yearling calf before the owner got to it.

Creeping Kate tried to imitate the "white squaws," and she wore her finery all the time, regardless of season, occasion, or place. When she headed her caravan in Taylor, she would decorate the high seat of her lumber wagon with a picture hat and flowing veil on her head, a rustling black taffeta dress, and kid gloves on her hands. If the weather was cold, she was wrapped in a mink coat that any New York society belle would have envied. Yes, the society belle would have envied the quality of the first grade mink fur, but she would not have desired the balloon-like cut of the coat, which sat on Kate like a tea cozy over a teapot or a tarpaulin over a hay mound.

The whole town knew when Creeping Kate arrived in town; she would halt her caravan in the main street and then start looking for Abram. Everyone in town would look for him too because they knew Kate would not do business with anyone unless he would oversee the transaction. Her past experience with Pete and his shady business trades meant that the cleverest and trickiest scoundrels would get the best of the deal. Father seemed to be the only one she truly trusted. He would buy her hides, pay her in silver dollars, and then go with her from store to store to see that she got her full money's worth in anything that took her fancy. Every storekeeper welcomed Kate with an overflowing enthusiasm, and she seemed to expect it. Here was a chance to sell their highest priced goods and the "white elephants" that stuck in their showcases.

A few yards of silk or satin did not satisfy Kate. She bought the whole bolt. She would clean up on the candy counter and shoes, and it would be several days after that before the grocery store could get in a new supply of candy and gum—even longer before boots and shoes could come from St. Paul. Kate did not camp like the other Indians but had a large tourist tent from Montgomery Ward and Co. that housed her and her family and a windbreaker tent for her horses. Her camping stove and utensils were the most modern, but her cooking was much like the Indian style. Kate left every one of her silver dollars in Taylor for safekeeping, and when she was ready to return to her claim, everyone gave her a cheering send-off. It was, "So long, Kate!" "Good-bye, Katie; come again, Katie," and then a lone voice yelled, "Who is better than Creeping Kate?" and another voice responded, "No one, damn you."

As her caravan went over the hill and out of sight, the crowd would still be yelling, "Three cheers for Kate!" And as she would disappear out of sight, they would let out wilder cheers with, "Three cheers for us! There's nobody like us!"

Berry had an Indian story, which he delighted in telling the Easterners. He would lean back in his chair in the hotel office and hold a lit cigar between his two first fingers. He could not smoke the cigar because just a few puffs would make him deathly sick, but he liked to toy with it as if he was just about to smoke it.

"The Sioux Indians are good Indians," he said, "but some of those bucks, both young and old, look wicked enough to scare the devil and all the imps of satan! There is that young buck, Scalp Face, a powerful looking fellow, and his face is so scarred from his forehead to his chin that it looks more like a patch of furrowed ground than a face! He understands and talks a little English too. Once I said to him, 'Where you fight, Scalp Face, to get all this?' and I pointed to his scarred face. He answered with a sort of a proud air: 'I no fight; I good Indian! This is white man scalp knife!' and then he pulled a sheathed razor out of the pocket of his buckskins. When I looked closely at the results, I didn't doubt his word. That Indian had been trying to shave his beardless face with a razor and had hacked it almost off."

## Young Man's Butte

While Taylor was a prairie town, it did not lay on a flat plain, but the whole surrounding country exhibited a gracefully waving surface, swelling and sinking with an easy slope and no angular elevations. Wherever you stood you felt that you were in the center of this vast plain with perfectly curved outline marked upon the sky—such a distant horizon line that showed that the earth was round, and your imagination could picture it flat too. There was a break in the eastern skyline, a well-known landmark, and a picturesque elevation that was called "Young Man's Butte."

The word *butte* is derived from a French word, handed to the West by the early French settlers. In the French language it identifies the object to which it refers. It is such a good word that we cannot find another in the English language that would be its precise equivalent. The name "butte" is applied to the detached hills and ridges that rise at intervals on the prairies and are too high to be called hills and not high enough to be called mountains.

Young Man's Butte was situated about seven miles east of Taylor, between the towns of Richardton and Antelope. It was on this skyline that we could see the smoke of the westbound train on the Northern Pacific Railroad as the train was going into town. There was always that moment when the train would pass the butte and the smoke seemed to be erupting from a giant crater, like a young Vesuvius. This point marked the time when the westernbound travelers at the hotel would get their luggage together and saunter on up to the station. This point also marked the time when everyone in Taylor, who was just hanging around looking for excitement, would make for that station platform just to see the train come in and gape at all the people on it. This brought the East to the West and the West to the East!

We learned a great deal about Young Man's Butte when two very dignified, bewhiskered men stopped off at the hotel on their way to the West Coast. They represented the American Antiquarian Society. One was a craniologist, and the other was a glacialist. They aroused a great deal of curiosity among the Taylorites, and it was difficult for Father to explain their mission.

He would say something like this: "They are two professors who dig around in the same place all day. Both see something different that is of value to science!" They rented Father's horse and buggy and spent most of their time at Young Man's Butte.

Professor Michael Tooley unearthed bones of human skeletons many feet below the surface. The bones were in a lying position, having never been disturbed since interment. The length of time had corroded most of the bones, so they crumbled in his hand when exposed to the air, and some were petrified. Arrowheads, wampum, and small beads were found near the bones, but his greatest joy came when he extracted from the earth the cranium of an Indian. He brought the gruesome thing back to the hotel and carefully wrapped as if it were a precious diamond. He showed it to us, pointing out the forehead with its truly peculiar and imposing flat receding slant, and then he said, "See, it has a sad falling off behind!"

I remember Father looked at it and remarked, "Yes, it has a sad falling off all around; it seems to me that such a head could turn edgewise in a hurricane and break the vacuum! Now I know why the Indian always turns his profile to you!" That was not the end of that Indian skull. Professor Tooley took it to his bedroom, and there it was immersed in his washbowl in a chemical glutinous substance to preserve it, if possible, and strengthen the piece in its entirety. The girls refused to clean his room while the skull glared at them from the washbowl. Mother was not afraid.

The antiquity of Young Man's Butte never failed to arrest the attention of visitors from far and near. They all agreed that centuries must have elapsed since this vast pile of earth was thrown up from the plain.

Professor Eugene Sarpy found the geological proof of the age of Young Man's Butte by digging in the same holes with Professor Tooley. He told us that the butte was a freak formation of uncertified boulder clay and interglacial deposits left in this form during the glacial period. He found proof, beyond a doubt, that this was the terminal moraine of the last ice sheet that swept over this region.

Sarpy was as delighted over his discovery as Tooley was with his half-petrified Indian skull, and while Tooley was filling his bedroom with human bones, Sarpy was carrying into his bedroom large boxes of hardened clay and smooth stones, which he said were "ice-worn." He even brought back a boulder, which was all that the two men could lift and carry in the buggy. His room was so filled with glacial dirt that the girls just had to give up trying to clean it until he shipped his collection to the Antiquarian Society. They did not complain about this, while they stood in awe and fear at the door of Tooley's room.

There is a story connected with Young Man's Butte that accounts for its name: In the early pioneer days, a family was driving west in a covered wagon, and their young son died en route. He was buried here, at the very top of this highest peak—the only monument they could give him. They could always find this place and came back to him. The two professors did not disturb the grave on top, which was marked by a stone. They were only unearthing the secrets, which nature held for them in the bowels of North Dakota's best-known landmark, Young Man's Butte.

*Chapter Four -*

# "Vive le Percheronne" Filly and the Gypsies

As my memory goes back to the Indians, I recall the most enjoyable gala days of my childhood: three wonderful, spectacular, popcorn and peanut days spent in Mandan at the Morton County Fair, helping Father exhibit Vive (our thoroughbred Percheron Filly). Vive was the most intelligent horse we ever owned and the most beautiful piece of horseflesh to ever strut the prairies. Father said that Vive must have her chance in society and make her debut at the fair, in the state entries. His interest in thoroughbred horses and sheep was quite noticeable.

It was Juttan who first aroused Father's interest in the fair. The Indians from our reservation were going to meet the Indians from Fort Yates and the Cannon Ball. They were all prepared to put on a big show with war dances, scalping raids, and a revival of all Indian traditions and customs. The advertising said that it would be "hair-raising" and "breathtaking" to see the struggle of the white man with the redskins in a tomahawk battle and a razed log cabin.

Vive was our big excuse for attending a fair in Morton County as our Stark County fair in Dickinson did not offer a state award for the best-bred filly. They had only to look at Vive to know that she was a thoroughbred of the purest stock, but Father did not have a scrap of paper to prove this. There was no record of her dam and sire in any studbook. Father came across Vive by chance; she was his reward for poking his nose in the horse business of some wandering gypsies who had camped on the outskirts of Taylor a year before.

Father liked the gypsies because of their lightheartedness and courtesy, their intense family affection, and their great love for all dumb creatures. He admired them because they were so quick and versatile; they readily adapted themselves to any state of life. He said that where there was so much innate good and such tender compassion that the outer character would have to express it. He would also remark that he had gypsy tendencies and gypsy longings in his own heart, and that if he did not have three "dependakins" on him, he would join the happy roving Romany band. Mother would even tell us to keep our eye on our papa while the gypsies were in town as "he might go traipsing off with that frazzled caravan! He had his fortune told already."

The day the gypsies left, Father came home with Vive. She did not have that name then; she was just a sad, forlorn undernourished little colt when he first got her, with big hoofs and knotty legs and a mangy gray coat that looked like a clay pack on a horse-skeleton frame. The gypsies had not bred the colt nor would they tell where they got her, so Father did not ask any questions. Father excused the gypsies; he explained, "They did not steal this little colt! I'll bet its father and mother had gone to the races, so the little 'gauntling' joined the gypsies!"

The name came later when a Frenchman stopped at the hotel on his way to the coast. He was having his dinner in the dining room. When he looked out of the window and saw our dapple-gray filly calling us from the back door, he gave one look at the horse and then threw up his hands in great glee as if he had found a long-lost relative, "Ah, *oui, oui, vive le Percheronne!*" He said this over and over, and tears came in his eyes. We could not forget the phrase, so we called her "Vive le Percheronne," but we called her "Vive" for short. She would answer to the full or partial name.

Francois Janisse pronounced her a thoroughbred from French ancestry. He told us about his home in northern France, where his father raised this breed of large, beautiful, and dapple-gray draft

## "Vive le Percheronne" Filly and the Gypsies

horses. François stopped off again at the hotel on his way back to St. Paul just to see Vive. She had broadened out now to her full growth, and she had a poise and grace as if she was aware of her great beauty.

Getting Vive ready for the fair was about the same as preparing a debutant for her debut in society or a prima donna for the Met. Everyone in the hotel—and it seemed that everyone in town—was interested and determined that "Vive le Percheronne" would carry the honors of the state for Taylor. Samuel Buel had complete charge of her grooming and gave instructions what to do. Her dapple-gray coat looked silvered-sheen satin with all the markings brought out from light to dark shades. Her mane was long and heavy and hung in a graceful fringe on her neck, and her bang added to the beauty of her face. Her tail was a silver plume that hung to her trimmed fetlocks, and no cruelty had to be exercised to give it that high-flung sweep. By this I mean that the upper vertebra of her tail was not broken to give the high arch that horse fanciers must have at all costs. Nature gives it if man would only be merciful.

Samuel would give Vive her freedom for exercise, and she would run around in circles and up over the hills and then come back to her stable, where her oats and mash would be waiting for her. While she was a draft horse and unusually large in size, she was lithe and graceful and looked like a silver streak on the prairies, her mane and tail tossing in the wind, a symphony of rhythm in motion.

Vive was broken to saddle, bridle and bit, harness, and buggy and broken just by Father's gentle manipulation and handling of her gently so that nothing ever hurt or frightened her. She did not object to anything we did and seemed to enjoy all the extra grooming in preparation for the fair.

We rode to Mandan in a stock train; Vive occupied a padded stall where she was well protected from any hurts or bruises.

Father stayed in the stall with her and had a nice little padded bench to sit on. I rode in the caboose (the conductor's car on the end of the freight train), and it was the most thrilling ride of my life. It was an ecstasy that can only come once in a human life. I was beside myself with an overwhelming happiness that transported me so far above my surroundings that I thought I was riding in a golden coach to a faraway castle. I was a beautiful golden queen with a silver charger!

That Morton County fair was pronounced the best fair that was ever held on the West Missouri slope. The weather was bright, sunshiny, and clear—ideal for October. Thousands of people from every section of the county came to see the show as well as people from adjoining counties and different sections of the state.

It was a farmer's and rancher's fair, and this phase was greatly emphasized. This was the best place for them to see what their neighbors were doing and what creative ingenuity was happening all over the state. It gave them an insight into the new methods whereby they could improve their own products and their stock.

There were the acrobats, the clowns, the band, and all that goes into making a fair. There were horse races, cowboy relay races, and an Indian relay race. The Indians were the outstanding feature of the fair, and they put on many a thrilling and realistic exhibition.

## The Deadwood Stagecoach

The famous Deadwood stagecoach was filled with people and held up by two masked hootin' shootin' cowboys and then finally attacked by a band of half-naked, befeathered, and war-painted Indians. They gave their Indian war whoops and fired blank shells and also made wild passes with bows and arrows. The Deadwood stagecoach would come out victorious, and the grand finale would be the burning of the Wells Fargo Express Office, which had been erected on the prairie. The cowboys came to the rescue, and as the embers of the conflagration were dying out, the show would close for the evening.

One big attraction of the Indian village was a very attractive tepee with a big placard in front, which read, "See the Big Show, 10 cents." Big Show was an Indian baby who was born the first day of the fair. The famous "Rain in the Face" had a teepee in the Indian village. "Rain in the Face" would hold "Big Show" and let you take their picture with your camera for ten cents. The newborn baby looked very husky, and his mother was a very lively young squaw. The pangs of travail among the Indians were only regarded as a natural incident in their life, and civilization had not yet commercialized on their rights.

Through the three days of the fair, "Vive le Percheronne" had been one of the greatest attractions in the stock exhibit. Her stall was silver and royal blue to bring out her own silvered beauty: a background of blue sky with a silver star. Banners and curtains of bunting draped the entrance. Vive posed and strutted and was so gentle and friendly that every man, woman, and child had given her a pat or let her nuzzle them with her sensitive velvet nose.

Vive received the top honors, and her blue-ribbon honor covered a lot of territory: the state of North Dakota. She also received a paper that would answer as a pedigree, not with a long list of ancestors but with a record that would give her a straight title to the pure-blood Percheron in Perche, France, and her name remained the same: "Vive le Percheronne."

Father had many offers for Vive; buyers were bargaining with each other, but he had no intentions of selling her. Our last night at the fair, he came to a very quick decision, and it was humane and right. He would sell Vive to a Mr. Maxwell of the Maxwell Percheron Stables in Centralia, Illinois.

When he first told me, I started to cry, and then he cried too. Then he explained why he must sell: "You see, Dotty dear, Vive is too big of a horse for us to use at home. We started with a little sick colt, and now we have a sort of an elephant-horse on our hands. Mr. Maxwell has been around her every day, and she has grown to like him; in fact, she calls to him just as she does to me when he comes in the stable. He has a horse ranch of just such heavy draft horses, and our Vive will have little colts and be very happy there."

I could see Father's viewpoint right away. Maple and I had always pictured Vive with a little colt that we could pet and help her raise, but a hotel and its small grounds were no place to raise horses—especially such big horses. I understood the whole situation, and I knew that this was not an easy decision for Father to make. I must help him.

We did not say good-bye to Vive; we just let Mr. Maxwell take over her care, and we kept out of sight but watched her from outside the stable. We saw that she was happy and trusted and loved her new master, but sometimes she would listen and then raise her head and give that long whinny that was her call for Father. It was so heartbreaking to pull away. Father would say, "She's got horse sense and human sense, and she knows we've deserted her, but there's no other way, Dotty; we must go home without her!"

We had another trial to face now. We had to break the news at home. By the time we arrived in Taylor, we braced up and made up our minds that we would not look dejected, so we started out with this story. Father put on a brave front and told everybody, "I sent Vive down to a horse ranch in Illinois to raise some colts! I can't go in the horse business here, but when you fellows want draft horses, I'll send after a carload." Mother and Maple got the truth afterward, and they grieved quietly with us for a while, but later, when a letter came from Mr. Maxwell telling us how happy Vive was in her new surroundings, we felt reconciled and happy too.

Often in our dreams that gorgeous silver filly would come back to us, and we would greet each other in the morning with, "Who do you think I dreamed about last night?" The answer would always be, "Oh, I know—Vive le Percheronne."

*Chapter Five -*
# The Tumbleweeds of North Dakota

Only those who have lived on the western prairies have seen the rolling, tumbling tumbleweeds racing across the plains like pursued wild things. During the hazy Indian summer days and through the autumn until the winter snowfalls, thousands of tumbleweeds are blown back and forth over thousands of acres of treeless land. They stop only when some barrier checks their tumbling advance, and there they wait for a reverse wind to release them and start them off in another direction.

The sight is fascinating, even to a land-bound Westerner. My childish imagination used to see them as galloping wild horses pursued by cowboys with sporting whirling lassos riding pinto ponies. With gentler winds, I would imagine that they were herds of mountain goats or black sheep seeking shelter. Strong regular winds rolled them across the plains like troops of marching soldiers. Hurricanes from the Rockies that came down through Medicine Hat drove the tumbleweeds like a powerful mongrel horde driven by a ruthless master. On quiet, balmy days, the tumbleweeds rested wherever they landed: piled high against fences, houses, barns, hay, and straw stacks, and they would fill the ravines and gullies. They were all waiting for the prairie winds to give them new life to go on and on.

The tumbleweed is a bushy, prickly plant that grows from one to five feet in diameter. Its root is too small for its large ball-like proportions, and at maturity the wind can easily loosen it from its anchorage in the soft sandy soil. Tumbleweeds were called Russian thistles on the prairies because the early Russian immigrants brought the seed over in their luggage, and once the seed got started, it spread rapidly. It has no nutritional value, and the farmers and ranchers are constantly fighting to eradicate it from their lands.

Tumbleweeds made glorious playthings for the children on the western plains. Maple and I would chase them over the hill and meet them on their return trip. We would build them into a wall and make playhouses and pile them high on a fence north of our barn to make a windbreak and a snowbreak for the winter. We would tie bright pieces of calico in the center of the prickly weed to identify it and then watch for its return.

Sometimes we would write notes and put our name and town on them. We were not the only ones sending messages via tumbleweed. The cowboys on the plains would put their name and address on a good sturdy weed and hope to find lovelorn maids to cheer their lonely lives.

Father said that it was a joke to say that a cowboy's life was lonely when he has more excitement in a day than an Easterner in a month of holidays. He said, "They live such full lives. If they're not full of rotgut, they're full of potgut, and either way, they're a 'happy-go-fetch-it' bunch with no time on their hands to be lonesome cowboys."

Redheaded Scott Mason, of the Alkale-Creek Ranch, found his redheaded wife through a "Tumbleweed Matrimonial Bureau," as Scott called it. He would tell his story like this, damning everything: "You see how it was. I got up one mornin' and saw a damn fool tumbleweed stick right in front of my damn little ole bunkhouse window. I went to loosen the damn fool thing an' thar wuz a note a hidin' in the center. Thar wuz a blue ribbon a holdin' the damnedest-lookin' lil' piece o' paper. On the paper was the name of the foolish redheaded Marvelly Shoup; she lived way out in that lil' ole town of Pocatello, Idaho. I was the biggest fool. I wrote to her, an' I can't write worth a damn. But she answered it!" And

Scott would mop his face with his bandana handkerchief and slide down in his chair completely licked.

"So one prairie tumbleweed changed the whole course of your life, Scott?" Father commented.

"Yep, that one damn tumbleweed jus' tumbled me right out of a life of sittin' easy to the damnedest tumble jumble existence ya ever heard tell of! Marvelly just tumbled every damn thing out of the ole ranch house and settled me down thar with the goldarndest new fandangled things ya ever saw. She said she wants a family too, so we're producin' like a pair o' jackrabbits, Pocatello-style, I guess!" And Scott would slide down on his backbone until he almost sat on his neck as he went on damning things.

Scott and Marvelly's five children followed each other into this world just as fast as nature could handle the situation. The kids were all good looking, and the strangest thing about them was their hair. The first boy had deep rich auburn hair, and as each one came, the shade became lighter, until the fourth, a little girl, had pale golden hair, and the last, little Albie, was a true albino.

It had gotten so that when anyone would say, "Marvelly has another baby!" the question would be, "Is the red hair still fading?" At one Fourth of July celebration, a cowboy remarked when he saw Scott and Marvelly lined up with their five little offspring, "Nice bunch of little Mason jars you got there! Seems to me you're runnin' out o' pigment, Scott—clean out o' pigment!"

Marvelly was holding little Albie, and she smiled as Scott answered, "Yep, we're out o' the damn pigment! This is our last o' the tumbleweed—the very last sprig, I'm tellin' you!"

A nicer, better-behaved group of children were never raised on prairie soil, and to this day, North Dakota has had many occasions to be proud of them.

Tumbleweeds are the most suggestive of people and particularly the people of the western states who have been blown westward by the winds of chance.

There are the strong, invincible characters that readily find a foothold, and when they do, they hold on tenaciously against all obstacles and all interference from outside sources. They are the reliant, self-confident citizens who make the country's very backbone.

Abram was such a tumbleweed character. He was positive and dominated in every situation. He would never accept a negative suggestion in his mind, and with his staunch faith in all his convictions, he made his cherished dreams come true. He made our dreams come true by his very forceful, affirmative assertions, working in the cosmic realm; but he was quite unaware of the power he swayed or of the source of that power. Abram had so many admirable traits. He was like a child in his enjoyment of life, and this gave him the viewpoint of simplicity and balanced his broader, rounder viewpoint with wisdom and prudence.

He dramatized every incident of his life, no matter how trivial. To Father, life was truly a stage and everyone an actor or an actress. He always played the leading role on his own little stage, and the lines he read were piquant with studied truths.

There are other tumbleweed people who are timid and shrinking, afraid to battle the storms of life. They avoid all conflicts and seek a refuge, a place of safety and seclusion, where the winds of chance can blow over them but cannot sweep them from their strongholds. They are like the tumbleweeds that are caught in the gullies and ravines. They are the "yes" men and women who overcrowd every community, so spineless, tiresome, and inconsistent.

## Tragedy on the Slopes of the Rio Grande

Still another type of tumbleweed people are those who are blown hither and thither by every passing wind. The stronger currents drive them back again over the same ground, and they make no advancement in life. The West is made up of such tumbleweed characters—where life is so large. Thinking of them all in this light, there is one character that was blown back and forth from the Missouri Valley to the Rio Grande in the southern Rockies and never found a foothold. This was Martin Shelby, and everyone called him Mart.

When he came to Taylor, it was like a great gust of wind from the north. The largeness of his person, the freedom of his every action, and his inch of purpose, all mirrored his indomitable spirit. When you heard someone say, "Mart's in town again!" you did not think of it as news. You *felt* that he was in town, so strong was his personality.

Mart had a claim of 160 acres that bordered on Taylor's south town site. He built a shack with a lean-to, dug a well, and tried to live on it as much as Uncle Sam required. Mart had a sort of private business: he did not profess to be a horse doctor or an animal doctor, but he was a private practitioner of veterinary medicine and surgery. If he was a real "vet" and had his degree, he did not boast of it or display his diploma in Taylor, but his animal cures and animal surgery were short of miraculous.

Abram said that Mart was more than a veterinarian. He was a humanitarian, and his doctrines and principles far outweighed those that are measured with the calculating rod of diplomas and degrees. Father and Mart formed a close friendship because their love and understanding of animals made a close bond.

Mart felt that he had a heaven-sent job on the prairies. When the winter winds would come down from the Rookies, like a war-god of impelling stature, and drive the storm-caught beasts to the ravines and gullies for shelter and protection, Mart would ride the prairie trails day and night looking for any hapless animal that was caught in the maelstrom of the elements. He worked for all the ranchmen.

If he could help the animal to life, he was ready with his kit of implements, and then he would drive it or carry it to the nearest ranch. If death were the only release, he would put a quick end to all suffering with a sure-aimed bullet from his trusty thirty-four.

We all welcomed Martin at the hotel. He would rough it just so long and then felt that he must get a little closer to the hearts of men. He would ride in on his horse Sandy, a sorrel gelding, and leave the check rein down while he went about town. Sandy would follow him and stand outside the building, so everyone knew where Mart was "hanging out."

Sandy centered all of his affection on Mart. Father liked to tease him about it. He would make remarks jokingly. Once he said, "Martin, if you had a woman who loved you as devotedly as Sandy does, why, you'd be about loved to death!"

This seemed to strike a sensitive chord in Martin's heart. He turned to Father, anguish in his eyes—and then tears. His voice was trembling. "Oh God, Berry, I had a woman...who loved me... more than words can tell...more than life can fathom! That's why I can't settle down! That's why the night winds call us down to the Rio Grande!"

They were in the hotel office, and then Mart put his head in his hands and broke down and cried—really sobbed until his great frame shook. "I'm sorry, Martin, I didn't know! My joking tendencies always get me in hot water." Father apologized. "You can be grateful and thankful at that, Martin. I always believe the saying, 'It is better to have loved and lost than never to have loved at all!'"

Martin and Father sat up late that night, after all the guests had gone to bed, and Martin sobbed out the tragic story of his one and only love—a story that sounded more fictional than real. He told Father of his first visit to the big ranch on the slopes of the Rio Grande, the "El Chaco." A foot disease had started in their cattle, and it was six months before he could eradicate it entirely. "The six happiest months of my life, Berry—an ideal layout for a ranch. And Orion Tilson was a man like you: educated and with a high degree of culture. He brought everything that was worthwhile and desirable to his own secluded paradise. It was all wildly beautiful, but it was a treacherous country where a narrow belt of buttes would rise abruptly from the plains and have precipitous sides and flat tops."

He went on explaining that Tilson's cattle were in the thousands: "We never could count them to a nose, but the hoof disease only affected a few that had contracted it over the border, so I readily overcame that, but I had to inspect every head of cattle on that ranch!"

"Go on," said Father, "I understand. Inspecting thousands of head of cattle kept you busy for a long stretch of time! Who was the girl?"

"She was Orion Tilson's daughter, Berry. I heard she was home from an Eastern college, but it was weeks before I got a glimpse of her, and then…well…we just fell in love with each other on sight and tried to be together as much as possible after that. Loyia was a horsewoman, an outdoor-kind-of woman and interested in every animal on her father's ranch. An Eastern college had not changed her or made a mincing manikin out of her to wear clothes nor had it made a dawdling puppet out of her to exploit her father's millions."

Father laughed knowingly, "She was quite a paragon, Martin; that type is rare for a college girl. I remember when you came back here at that time to start plowing on the claim. We all teased you about your hilarious spirits. I told Annie, then, that there was a woman in it! Then you went back to the Rio Grande, and Mart, you've never been the same man since. I've often wondered what happened. But I knew if you wanted to tell me, you would!"

Father told me this story after I had grown to young womanhood. He said that it was some time before Martin could go on with his story that night. Just living again in the memory that brought it back to him so vividly, he was overcome with emotion, and his pent-up heart longingly gave into his feelings in a flood of tears. Father said that he never saw a strong man so utterly broken in spirit and yet fighting so hard to go on with life bravely.

Mart finally got hold of himself and went on with his story. "Loyia and I had ridden all over that range many times. We knew all of that rocky country, cut up with rocky ravines and fissures. Our horses knew every foot of the ground and were sure-footed and would not take any chances.

"They knew their trails and could easily leap from some of the short cliffs. That day, Berry, we were riding toward the ranch house on the Rio Grande side. Loyia was pointing out the beauty of the steep bluffs of red and white sandstone rock. We were laughing like two children and said that the scenery about us was medieval. We imagined that all about us were fortresses and castles and before us lay a drawbridge spanning the chasm of the Rio Virden. Loyia was laughing and said, 'Do you see the drawbridge, darling? My slaves are letting it down, so we will cross before our enemies overtake us!' I don't know what happened then, Berry!

"My mind was blank to what was happening. I don't know if Loyia turned her horse off the trail to the edge of the precipice or if the horse swerved, but horses don't swerve into danger; they sense danger! I don't know what happened! They left my side like a flash. I turned to see and looked toward the canyon bed and saw the bay pony standing with its feet braced within a foot of the very edge of that rock abyss. Loyia turned a complete somersault over his head and dropped into that mad rush of waters below! Her cry, Berry! Her cry of terror struck me dumb! She screamed just one word in a shrill tremolo, 'Marty!'

"Another cry rent the air, and that pony shrieked like the wild windstorm. I don't know why I did not throw myself in that chasm to be washed down with her to the Rio Grande! I don't know what I did for hours on those sandstone bluffs! I was there all night; the horses nuzzled me, but I was numb to all sense of feeling! All hope was useless; I could not leave the spot! I was a madman that night, utterly bereft of reasoning and thinking! No, it could not have been the force that swerved! Loyia did not want to die. Oh, God! No! She was quick and impulsive, and the pony was turned so near the chasm that he had to brace himself to keep them both from going over the ridge! Oh, God, Berry! In one second all I had in life was taken away!

"Tilson and all his men were out on the hunt, but the canyon road was the last one they thought of. We never found her body, Berry, so the ocean must be her grave! The Tilsons go on living; I go on living. We all go on living, and there is a lot to live for and a lot we must do. The animals that are unfortunate need me; suffering beasts need me! Loyia would want me to give my life to save the lives of animals. That would be the most I could do for her!"

The two men grew friendlier after that confession, and then they began to compare their ideas on religion. Martin felt very bitter toward life at times—when his sorrow weighed him down—and then he would declare that he hadn't an ounce of religion left. It was then that Father would always come forward with a pungent remark that was keen and caustic enough to break the barriers of thought and bring Mart back to a deep sense of outward living. They got so that they agreed on a day-by-day, livable religion. Neither of them belonged to any church or cult, nor did they believe in any creed, dogma or doctrine. Their thinking was as free as the winds from the west, and their minds were unfettered by any system of beliefs.

Mart would say, "I don't give a 'hoot' about the saving of my soul!"

Berry would answer, "I don't give two 'hoots!' If we have to surrender our freedom for the fear of damnation and of living in a sulfurous Hades, then our two souls would not be worth the trouble of saving." Then he would "Haw, haw! Just imagine a God of justice, a divine creator, stooping to these man-invented laws of the nation!" In their broad, answerable philosophy they had no place for a picayune God or a God who was running a manmade, commercialized heaven business through fear-appealing church activities.

"Now take this devil character!" And Father loved to express his ideas and build up on all the old-time church beliefs. "The devil hangs around to pick up all of God's unmanageable cases. I guess one prick with that two-tined fork jumps them right into that boiling cauldron of pitch! The churches don't even make their heaven inviting, so there must be another heaven for unbelievers like us."

## Worship on the Prairie

From overhearing such conversations, I conceived my ideas of creation, and in my childish mind there were two distinct Gods running two distinct religions. There was the religion of the churches, which must be powerful with so many followers. Then there was the other religion, which Father and Mart talked about, but they did not go inside of a church, nor did they have any followers in Taylor or any place that I knew of. They worshiped God as a great all-prevailing principle of truth and all knowledge. I got strange, mixed-up ideas of religion.

Their church was out on the lengthened lands, under the vastness of the heavens—the blue canopy of the sky. Mart said that he had another church in the craggy depths of the "Cascade Grotto on the Rio Grande, where the stars looked down from opal skies." He said that it was only in outdoor churches that one could feel akin to every God-made thing. I heard Father say, "Out there God talks to man, and what has man got to say? Nothing—but listen to the voice of his creator!"

I tried to make the great outdoors my church. Over the hill, east of the hotel, I could crouch in the grass and listen—listen for the voice of God. His voice did not come from the sky or the ground or even through the tall buffalo grass. I did not pray because Father had said, "Listen!" Then the day came when I decided that Father's God and Mart's God did not come to me, and I did not have the God of the Methodist church or the Lutheran churches of Taylor, so I must be a heathen. I classed myself with the heathens of the world; until I learned differently one day.

The Methodists of Taylor held their church in our hotel dining room, and that was always a very exciting day for Maple and me. Not a detail escaped our eyes. The congregation would gather from far and near, dressed in their Sunday raiment, rather somber and dark. Mother would dress in her best and join them in one of the front seats so she could lead in the singing. Maple and I would hover around the door from the hallway. We were self-appointed ushers. We would take our friends up front because they were rather hard of hearing. Maple said that we must take those who "paid" the most to the front seats and those who give the least way back in these board seats, "so maybe, they'll feel more like supporting the minister after they sit here and tire their sit-upons."

It was Maple and I who would pass the collection plates—two large silver platters. The silver dollars would ring well, and just from the ring one could hear what each "Methodisty" would drop on the plate. When five silver dollars would drop at once the clang would be so great that nearly every head would turn to see the cheerful giver. A fifty-cent piece would make a sort of an apologetic ring, and when a quarter was dropped, the "ping" was so weak that nearly every head would turn and look at each other with a raised eyebrow or a twitch of the mouth. Maple and I would look across at each other, so it got so that the quarters were scarcer. Maple said, "Afraid to say 'Ping?'"

Neither Father nor Martin nor many of the New Jerseyites attended the church services. Father was always unusually busy in the office at that time. Once I went in and asked him if he wanted to give anything to the church, and he answered, "Why, I have given my share; why, I've given my dining room Scot-free! Now what are you giving?"

I had never thought of giving any money, and then I seemed to know why: "Oh, I'm not giving anything! That's why the church takes money—to help the heathen, and I'm a heathen, so I don't have to pay!"

Maple always laid her fifty-cent piece on the plate so that it did not ring. She had explained to Mother, "That's what my inner conscience tells me to pay, and I also help them. I serve as an usheress!" Mother would drop a dollar, and sometimes two or three would ring on the platter. Mother gave to every good cause and never argued the reasons with herself.

Dickinson had several denominational church buildings. Gladstone had a Methodist edifice, and they usually sent their preacher to preside at the Taylor meetings, and sometimes a traveling minister would hold a week of revival meetings to stir up the religious sentiments of the backsliding Methodists. Father always donated his dining room for the meeting place, and the church people looked after the care and comforts of the visiting ministers.

The cowboys always referred to the preacher of God's words as the "sky pilot." This name always made my picture of a sky heaven more vivid and real and quite an intriguing place to think about, but I was quite determined that I did not want to go there. Maple and I would listen intently to the minister, and we would play church with all the solemn fervor of a presiding elder. I would open our play church by reading a hymn in a very impressive manner:

>   Help us to help each other, Lord,
>   Each other's cross to bear.
>   Let each his daily aid afford
>   And feel a brother's care.

Neither Maple nor I could sing with any resemblance of a tune, but this did not keep us from singing any hymn or any song to our own original composition of music. We inherited our nonsinging voices from Father, and he seemed quite proud to be different from other folks. He was absolutely tone-deaf and would boast that he could not tell the tune of "Yankee Doodle Dandy" from "Home Sweet Home."

Maple and I were different. We knew the various tunes, recognized them readily, and thought that we could sing them, but our modulation of pitch sadly lacked the right inflection, and we were happily unconscious of it. I would listen intently to every word the ministers preached and try to convey the message to Father when he would ask: "What did the good reverend say to the good people today?"

I would climb up on his knee to tell him: "He said that you can't find God in church, even if you go to church for years and years. Why, you can't find God if you do more work than all the angels in heaven, and there are thousands of angels! He said that you can't find God by asking questions of anybody else or even by reading about God in the Bible!"

Then Father asked, "How did he tell you to find God?"

"He said that you just had to keep on asking the Lord to keep on making you better and better in your heart 'til there is no more bad life in you. Then you'll be good enough to find God and listen to God's word!"

I told just what I understood from the sermon, but the great question in my mind was which God was working for me—the sky pilot God or the God who got inside of me like Father's God?" Many amusing incidents happened in our church meetings in the hotel dining room, and they are outstanding in memory because Father's great sense of humor made him see a funny side to every situation.

One Sunday in early fall, a Reverend Doty from St. Cloud, Minnesota, was holding special services to raise money for the depressed and unenlightened people of faraway countries. He announced his text in his sanctified, preachy voice: "In my father's house are many mansions."

He had scarcely read the words when there was a mumble from the back—the plank-and-box-made seats in the dining room. "That's a lie, hic! I tell you folks that's a lie, hic! I used to live in St. Cloud, and I know his father had a farm with three rooms and a lean-to. That's all! Sure as I'm a livin', hic! That's a lie! He ain't got many mansions!"

This was Ken from St. Cloud, who worked on a ranch there but who went to a booze spree every time he had a chance. Several pairs of hands dragged him out of the dining room and to the hotel porch, where the sharp west wind whisked a little clarity into his bemuddled brain. Someone told him that he had to apologize. So when the reverend walked out on the porch just in time to make the westbound train for Dickinson, he took hold of Ken's hand and said, "Keep the commandments brother, and sin not!"

Ken could not utter a word but shook the minister's arm like a pump handle. Then later, to those who had told him to apologize, he stammered: "Maybe he had mansions in his house; I was never inside!"

I recall vividly another sermon delivered by a Methodist reverend from "way back East." His words to the Taylorites were deep and searching yet affectionate and impressive. I do not recall his text, but he talked on "prayer." He urged his congregation to pray, to pray unceasingly. He said, "Hold a prayer meeting in your homes and bring your children up in the way of the Lord."

Maple and I knew all the Bible stories and all the Bible characters. We knew all the "begets," so we could recite them like a poem. "Abraham beget Isaac, etc." We had our own book, which

Grandma Berry had sent us from New Jersey: *The Bible in Picture Story*, and Mother would read the same stories to us from the Bible. Father would also attempt to tell us the stories and make them like living people of our day. They had the same problems, troubles, and disasters, and he would emphasize the fact that they brought everything upon themselves by their wrong thinking, wrong beliefs, and wrong living. He impressed upon us how they had to work out their own destinies, the same as we do today. Father believed implicitly in the divine laws of cause and effect, the law of retribution, which worked justly for the good and the bad. This was the way he would explain to us all the good and bad things that were happening in the world. Everything seemed so very clear when we could go to Father with our problems.

Jesus Christ seemed like a real and living person to us—a man who lived a long time ago who expressed God-like qualities. He taught all the people who would listen to Him to live their religion day by day. Father said that the life of Jesus was our measuring rod—the highest standard we had as an example of truthful living with a love for all humanity and an equal love for all lower creations—a love for all life because all that expressed life were a part of the God principle. Father took God right out of the sky and left no exalted deity to worship but a real, living, emerged and submerged God-spirit that pervaded the entire universe.

This did not seem real clear to me then, and because I did not have the sky pilot's God, I liked to class myself as a heathen, and I told Father, "If God wants me, he has got to make himself better known to me!"

And I remember Father's reply: "That's good; he'll get you to understand some day!"

We soon noticed that Martin Shelby came to the hotel when the church meetings were held in the dining room. He would not attend the services, but he would clink his dollar on the platter and sit in the office with Father. He would also wait for Maple and I to give our detailed account of all that happened and would laugh at our general sizing up of the stinginess of some of the "amen chorus." He and Father laughed heartily one time when Maple said, "This divine is preaching a very long sermon today because he is giving them the sincere milk of the word."

Father turned to Mart with, "Well, he'll just about be milked dry!"

Mart retorted, "As for me, there are times when I prefer condensed milk!"

There came a time when Martin Shelby left our section of the country. He pulled up stakes and went to the Rio Grande country to take charge of the "El Chaco" ranch. He came back once after that, but he was not the same Mart. The Taylorites said that he was "loco," but Father said that he was just living too much within himself and thinking of the one and only romance that had ever come into his life. He told Father that Loyia came to him in the night winds over the Rio Grande, and Father seemed to understand. My throat would tighten, and a tingling feeling would run up and down my spine when I listened to Mart talking in a low tone to Father something like this: "Those are rare moments, Abe, rare moments indeed when I am out on those craggy heights of the Rio Virden where Loyia went over the rocks. First music comes to me: soft, gentle Aeolian harmonies that the west wind creates in the lacy fronds on the river bank. There are times when there is a soundless silence and then the sound silence of the universe. Loyia comes to me then; I feel her nearness, and then I hear her voice far away and then near—soft and low and then in a high treble from the topmost crags. I can't tell her father and mother; they would not hear her voice. It is for me only that Loyia comes, and that's why I must live my days near that chasm in the southern Rockies."

Martin Shelby did not come back to Taylor again, and even his postal cards grew fewer and at last stopped. Father said he was glad that Mart did not come back: "He is uplifted with a happiness out there that the winds have taught him. He is experiencing one of the heart-easing miracles of the invisible world. He is a *tumbleweed* character who has at last found refuge in a new soil and is no longer buffeted by the winds of chance."

*Chapter Six -*
# Hotel Dining Room Becomes a Theater

Our dining room was the meeting place of every large gathering in Taylor. The new Jerseyites had formed a literary society that had been meeting in the schoolhouse. At first they had very informal meetings and discussed the latest books, but as they grew in numbers and had to accommodate members from the surrounding towns, our dining room was chosen for the literary rendezvous.

When Father was appointed program chairman, he said that the society was now large enough to promote enterprises, and it must bring more culture to the West. It must invite outside speakers and lecturers. The opportunity to try this came suddenly. Father received a circular stating that Alex A. Alexander of London was traveling from coast to coast in the United States and was available for the bargain price of one hundred dollars a program. He was very versatile and offered a wide range of subjects: music, drama, tragedy, comedy, monologues, sleight of hand, mystic or black magic, and choice of the whole Shakespearian repertoire.

A meeting of the literary board decided on *Hamlet* and an invitation to the public to attend, with tickets at one dollar per head to raise funds for the society's treasury. Announcements were made in all of the local papers of the adjoining towns, but the *Dickinson Press* gave the best front-page publicity. In the center of the front page was a most imposing picture of Alex A. Alexander, in costume of Hamlet, confronted with his father's ghost.

How this news did travel. The whole countryside wanted to see and hear what it was all about, even if they were not very literarily inclined. Temporary seats were arranged in the dining room to its full capacity, and Father began to doubt if even that would take care of the outsiders who were clamoring for tickets and asking him what kind of a show it was going to be.

Gil from Haliday always gets everything confused, so he thought a fellow named Shakespeare was going to impersonate a fellow named Alex A. Alexander. Father did not try to enlighten him but said that he didn't care which way it was as long as he gave a good performance. Gil was two days overdue at this ranch but decided to stay in Taylor another day to see "that Hamlet ghost, whatever it is."

There was always that very rough and rowdy element throughout the West, and they would become unmanageable after drinking the illegal rotgut whiskey, and then their great delight was to playfully shoot up the town. They were not evil in their intentions, but it seemed to be the only way to express their exuberant spirits. They were the cowboys who had drifted west seeking jobs, the influx from other states who had no settled homes—the human tumbleweeds who are ever blown back and forth by the winds of chance.

Father knew that he had this element to deal with. An unusual number were in town with their pockets full of silver, so he knew he had to be prepared for any surprises. He notified the sheriff of Stark County at Dickinson, Sheriff Jeb Morrison, that he needed a hand of the law to see that order and decorum were established at this first public meeting of the Taylor Literary Society. He knew that many would have to be rejected at the very doors, and his moral persuasion would not be strong enough.

The sheriff sent his number-one deputy, Josef Weiber of Dogtooth Hills homestead, and he was equipped with all authority to enforce the law. Everyone in Stark County knew Josef only as "Biceps Joe." He was an iron mountain of a man who seemed to be cut out from a giant pattern. He was over six feet tall and weighed around three hundred pounds.

## Hotel Dining Room Becomes a Theater

He would throw back his shoulders, pound his big hairy chest, and inform any gaping audience, "I am three hundred pounds of bones, muscle, and guts, and I can lick any three of y'ur best fightin' men." With that boast he would roll up his sleeves and take a stance, bending his right forearm to contract his great steel-banded muscles.

No one ever argued with Joe, but he was never serious—only when he represented the law as the county's number-one deputy. He would never offend or hurt anyone, but his happy-go-lucky disposition always suggested extravagant shiftlessness and a sunny gabble of Luxemburg, where he came from.

On the day of the lecture, the dining room was in readiness, with the doors of the office and the hall open and seating room made with planks laid on kegs. Biceps Joe took his place on the front porch and acted as a welcoming committee of one. He greeted everyone in an overly polite manner, bowing (and more bowing if it was a lady) or shaking hands with the man. When he saw any of the drunken rowdies coming toward the steps, he would walk forward to meet them and drawl out of the side of his mouth, "Vamoose, hombre, vamoose!" If they did not turn heel at once, he would swing his great arm into position with the biceps taut, ready for the punch. This was all the persuasion needed. Everyone knew that when Joe had ever given his special undercut, he had laid his victim out cold and it had taken hours of hot and cold water applications to bring the poor devil back to life.

The English speaker, Alex A. Alexander, was expected on the westbound afternoon train. I stood with Father on the station platform when the train arrived, and that platform was crowded with men, women, and children, even babies in arms. Here was a type of man the westerners rarely laid eyes upon. His manner was charming and his politeness overwhelming with a subtle dignity that held one at arm's length.

I could see that Father liked him from the first greeting, and Harvey, Gary, Vanier, Stephens, and all the New Jersey folks who were with us to meet him showed their sincerity in welcoming the Englishman. I liked him because he treated me like a grownup, and then when I walked close to him, he took hold of my hand as we walked down Main Street to the hotel.

He complimented us on our live, wide-awake little town so beautifully situated on the lengthened lands of the Middle West. "This is the land of the golden grain; here is where the earth grows splendid!" His eyes seemed to be taking in every detail along the way. Everyone greeted us with a "Howdy, Mister" and "Hello, Berry" and some with a "How are you doing, Dotty?"

Mr. Alexander smiled and said, "Ah, friendly little community. I should jolly like to live here."

Father assured him that it was a wonderful place, and one had only to mention the country to get Father enthused. "The air here gets in your blood, Mr. Alexander. The longer you stay, the better you like it." They both laughed, and then Father added, "I'm telling you that the future of North Dakota has a rainbow on it," and he agreed.

## Bodyguard for the Englishman

When we arrived at the hotel, Biceps Joe strutted across the porch to meet us, his chest heaved up like an inflated balloon and his great arms swinging at this sides like two weighted pendulums. He had looked rather neat when he had arrived in the morning, but now he was rather disheveled, his face red and perspiring, and his clothes wrinkled. Father and I knew that this meant that he had several encounters with the rowdies. But all was quiet now "on the Potomac" (our porch).

Mr. Alexander sized Joe up from head to foot, his head moving as his eyes took in Joe's full proportions, and as we walked up the steps, he remarked to Father in a side whisper, "My work! What

## Hotel Dining Room Becomes a Theater

a magnificent specimen of North Dakota manhood! What a product of the state! What a fine animal!"

That phrase remained with me. Was he really praising Josef Weiber? I had heard the cowboys speak of Joe as "a big hulk of brute strength," and his neighbors around Dogtooth Mills called him the "bull buffalo," and everyone said, "He's a devil of a man for fighting!" The Englishman was really admiring Joe.

Father introduced them: "Mr. Alexander, here is Josef Weiber, your bodyguard and our door tender. We call him Biceps Joe, and you can see the reason why." Then Father explained about the ruffians and why Joe was sent by the sheriff.

The Englishman extended his hand, and Joe grabbed it in his big ham-like palm. He must have squeezed to the point of pain as the poor Englishman winced a little and seemed very anxious to get his hand back.

"Right you are. Biceps Joe, a very befitting name! A cowboy bouncer, I take it! I have no fear of anything with you back of the door!" and Mr. Alexander gave Joe an assuring smile.

Joe was stepping from one foot to the other and loving all the time and attention. "I'm overjoyed and powerfully delighted to meet youse! Don't youse fear a thing! When I corral all the intellectuals in that eating room, I'll keep these dratted ignoramuses out! I'm decidin' who's goin' in and who ain't! It takes muscle convincin' here! I'm the law! I'm the law in Taylor today!"

When Mr. Alexander stood on the red-carpeted platform with the red draperies forming a rich background, he was another personality in another world. He looked over his mixed audience: faces of intellect and culture and faces of the peasant emigrants side by side. Easterners in the West and representatives from nearly every country in Europe, all eager and waiting for any diversion he could bring to them.

He toned his opening speech down to childlike simplicity and then impersonated the principle Shakespearean characters.

He made them come to life in real breathing men and women so that all could understand. He held his audience spellbound; they laughed and cried with him, felt every emotion, and expressed it with intense abandon. They breathed in pain with Hamlet; they suffered with the tempest-tossed Lear; and when Mr. Alexander enacted the wife in *Taming of the Shrew*, Seth nudged his wife, Sarah, and then she reached for his hand and held it. Father said afterward, "That was the taming of Sarah!"

Those who had never heard of Shakespeare before now had a perfect understanding of each character and something to take away with them. Had the speaker given them the entire role of Hamlet they would have become bored and squeamish, but his varied program produced a sympathetic, close fellowship and a great interest in the future of the Taylor Literary Society by the outside public.

Father sat in the office near the outside door, and I sat with him. During the program there would be a loud commotion occasionally, and Joe's commanding voice always seemed to bring quiet. Just as Mr. Alexander was giving us a summing up of the *Tempest*, the outer door was thrust open, and in came three staggering cowboys. Father knew them; harmless, would-be cowboys, who had a farm homestead in Flasher, so he just stood up and let them pass in.

They doffed their wide-brimmed sombreros and bowed toward the speaker. One of them swaggered forward while the other two stood near Father. Jake was the spokesman: "No o'fence, Mister. We jus' told Biceps Joe we wanted to take a look inside. We got here too late for your spiel. We don't mean any harm; we jus' want a look, that's all we want. We convinced ol' Bull Buffalo that we wanted a look." With that, the boys swept their ten-gallon hats to the floor in a deep bow and walked out and down the steps.

Father followed them out, and we could hear him say, "Hey, Josef, wake up! Don't tell me they knocked you out! Say, Joe, there's something weak in the law out here." Father knelt by the big hulk of brute strength. Biceps Joe was measuring his great length and breadth on the porch floor, and both of his hands were caressing his chin. Later, when Father was laughing about it, he said that the climax was greater than any that Shakespeare had ever written.

## Darwin's Book

There was a well-worn leather-bound book that rested in a niche in the whatnot that hung on the wall next to the large mirror in the hotel office. It was Darwin's *Origin of the Species*, and Father knew the theory from cover to cover and would delight to expound his views when he found anyone who welcomed a good debate. Some of the Jerseyites would argue with him to hear what he had to say, and many came in the office just to start an argument or debate on any subject.

Father liked to come out with some tongue-splitting phrases that would sometimes jar his listeners if they did not know when to laugh. Maple and I knew this and would watch for the different reactions. Father would pick up his *Saint Paul Daily* and give a great exclamation of surprise: "Well, well—what do you think about that? I had no idea it was that bad."

By that time everyone looked at him and gasped, "What is it, Berry? What's the news?"

Father would read from the front page, with the newspaper raised high so that no one could see his face and detect the twinkle in his eyes. "Why, the Reverend Dr. Crosby says that Darwin's hypothesis of the pangenesis involves several intangible subsidiary hypotheses. Now what do you think of that?" He always read it very fast in an excited tone.

The reactions were different. I remember when Lyman looked at Father and said, "Say, are you crazy, Berry, or are you just a damn fool?"

Our friend Ed said, "Oh, Berry, it's even worse than that, and it's very contagious if one compresses too much of that intellectual pemmican in his cerebral cranium. It leads to intellectual indignation."

The reaction of Matthias was nonplusing to Father and everyone in the room. Matthias would look up from his game of solitaire, raise his heavy eyebrows, frown over his glasses, and yell in his double-down bass voice, "To hell with the species; to hell with the fauna and the flora." Then he would bow his back and again lose himself in his game of cards.

Father had a Darwin lap story which he called "A Tale with a Tail." Maple and I knew the story well, but it always grew more interesting with his telling; little surprise would leak in. "Once upon a time, Mr. Darwin, a great English naturalist, went to jungle land to study the little monkeys. He caught some of them and took them in his home to watch them. He wanted to see if monkeys acted like people or if people acted like monkeys. One little monkey got away from him and went back to land jungle land, and all the other little monkeys gathered around him to ask questions.

"'What is man like?' 'What has man got?' 'What does man do?' The little Darwin monkey shook his head sadly and said, 'Poor thing, poor thing. He looks something like us, but he's sadly lacking. He has hands and feet, but they are such poor imitations of ours—so weak, so useless. He can walk and run, and some of them cannot run. He cannot run up trees as we do, and he cannot swing from branch to branch, the poor thing.'

"All the little monkeys felt so sorry for the poor man, who looked so much like them but who seemed so weak and helpless in the use of himself. They were brushing tears out of their eyes with coconut leaves when the little Darwin monkey continued: 'I have not told you the worst. He is absolutely, completely, entirely, yes, totally without a tail!' 'No, no, no!' Echoed every little jungle monkey in chorus. 'How can he get along without a tail?' 'He has to use his head to devise things—to make up for this lack,' said the little Darwin monkey. 'And some of the poor things have hardly got a head. It may look like a head, but it is useless to him, and he must depend on other men's heads.'

"Then all the little jungle monkeys sang in high glee, 'We have more than man, and man has nothing on us.' 'Oh yes, I must tell you,' said the little Darwin monkey. 'Man has only one thing that we have not got—only one thing.' 'Do tell us quickly. What has man got that we have not?' And the chorus from the trees was deafening. The little Darwin monkey looked very sad as he pronounced the words slowly: 'Man has *diseases*. Poor man!'"

"Is that all?" we would ask Father.

"Yes, that's all the monkey had to tell. Then all the monkeys jumped around and threw coconuts at each other to play ball." Father's dramatization of the story brought the meaning to us vividly, and our greatest sympathy was with "poor man."

Now I would like to add a sequel to the story of man's inhumanity to helpless sub-humanity. I mean, the devil-inspired practice of deliberately inflicting diseases upon sound and wholesome little monkeys from jungle land through inoculation with virulent matter or the feeding of unnatural substances to give them dire and dreadful diseases. If Father knew that it was being practiced to some degree at that time, he did not distress our minds with the knowledge.

The sequel of "A Tale without a Tail" would tell of the sadistic perversion of a powerful body of medical perverts who work secretly behind closed doors at the blackest of all Balch crimes: vivisection. Because the little jungle monkeys are so like humans, these denizens of evil have forced the virus of all their horrible diseases upon them under the guise of "helping humanity in finding a cure." How the gods must laugh, and how the monkeys can laugh at man because humans cannot hope to rule the world until they learn to be kind and gentle-minded about the beasts of the fields and the jungles.

## Chapter Seven -
# School Days in Taylor

Getting an education in the West was not such a difficult undertaking as the Easterners thought it would be. Grandma Berry had despaired of Maple and me making any grades in a "land of Indians and outlaws." It looked dubious to Father and Mother at first, but our education already started in New Jersey, and we were both very eager and apt pupils. Everyone was our teacher.

Father said that he knew we would get educated without half trying because as soon as we arrived in North Dakota he heard of two young men in Dickinson, "who had learned all they could in the schools here and had gone to Europe to learn more."

The Taylor schoolhouse was a neat little building on Front Street, near the section house, with one long room, which had carpenter-made seats and benches, a table desk, and a swivel chair for the teacher. There were blackboards on the wall and a drum-heater stove in the center of the room.

There was an entrance hall, which also had coat and hat hooks at different elevations to accommodate all ages. A long handmade bench held the water pail and dipper and a wash basin and soap dish. At the back of the schoolroom was a shed for coal and wood, broom and dustpan, and anything needed for the school's comfort. Here was everything needed for the material welfare of North Dakota's future citizens, and they were supremely happy and did not ask for more.

Maple and I went to school "when school kept." Each school season was three months long, and the number of seasons depended on the weather, but school was not continuous for teachers or pupils. Sometimes the teachers would make their home at the hotel, if they felt they could afford to pay four dollars and fifty cents a week. Every family wanted to board the teacher; it brought a nice influence into the home—besides the extra dollars.

Father was president of the school board and "hired and fired" the teachers, as Samuel Buell would tell anyone who asked. I remember when Father once had difficulty in finding a teacher for a winter term and then gave the position to Bertha Hillern, a pretty girl from South Heart, who hardly looked old enough to teach. She was very timid and not very keen on mathematics, and the older pupils soon found it out and delighted in asking her math problems until Bertha would break down in tears.

Enoch Leslie was the worst culprit at only fourteen. Enoch was a calculating wizard, but that was all that registered in his gray matter. Father made a visit to Enoch's home to tell him that he had to stop harrowing the teacher or leave the school. Enoch's father threatened Enoch with a rawhide beating if he didn't stop, and then he tried to apologize to Father for Enoch.

"Miss Hillern is a good teacher, Berry, but she ain't much of an arithmaticker, but she is a mighty fine grammarister, but that don't weigh nothing with Enoch! My Enoch knows figgers every way you put 'em: upside down, hine-side first, the goes-intos and the goes-out-ofs. I guess my wife marked him; she had a lawsuit over her butter and egg money and for nine months, with Enoch inside, she did nothin' but figger an' figger for discountin', then Enoch was born! His head is like a stone wall, nothin' else will go through it but figgerin."

"Well that explains it all," said Father, and he turned to Enoch. "You can stop your arithmetic or just go on by yourself, but try to get some grammar and geography and spelling. You'll need them all someday."

Father advertised in Eastern papers for teachers, and he found high-grade, well-educated women from the colleges and universities of the midwestern states. This brought a nice influence and new ideas into our little community. The teachers usually led in the social life of the town and aroused a musical and dramatic spirit in our literary society.

The West seemed to look upon school teaching as a woman's job, and the lengthened lands called for the strong arm of man, with muscles and sinews of steel. The West called for superior intellect and super brain power of man to take advantage of the unlimited possibilities of the land and climate and freedom. Women were doing the gentler tasks. Eric Arensen said, "Berry always hires teachers of the feminine gender, and he's just as good a judge o' school teachers as he is o' horses and hogs." The school superintendent was a man, and he could hold other offices or run a farm or ranch because any salary paid by the school board would not assure more than three square meals a day and a bed to sleep upon.

Doctor Stickney was county superintendent of schools for several years, and under his supervision the public school curriculum became far superior to that of many Eastern states. Thomas Elman later took over the office and kept the school system to the highest standard and aroused the interest for learning in both parents and pupils. Even the childless felt that they had some connection with the school.

Maple and I received part of our education by "playing school!" This game started when we were tiny tots in Chester, and Grandma and Grandpa Berry taught us to count and say our *A B Cs*, and Father and Mother continued the game in North Dakota. We would arrange our little table and chairs in schoolhouse order and have books, slates, pencils and crayons, a tablet of paper, and a carrying case for our school supplies. It could be in any room in the hotel that was convenient.

We would go through all the preliminaries of dressing for school, carrying our books, and, when Father or Mother would ring the bell, taking our seats and having the opening address by the teacher. Mother would usually lead with a song, "My Country 'tis of Thee" or the "Star Spangled Banner." If Father was the teacher, we would have a very nice speech, urging us to study hard and know our lessons well. He would say, "I would rather have this dunce cap get dusty and yellow from standing than to wear it out on your heads!" He had made a very high white paper dunce cap, and there were times when we would enjoy acting silly and dumb just to sit in the corner and wear the cap.

Our play lessons were not confined to school textbooks but included any of our pictures or reading books that Grandma sent us from New Jersey. As we grew older we were asked to do research work on any subject that aroused our interest or curiosity. Our home library was well stocked with good literature, and every Taylorite offered to lend us the books they had. We grew up familiar with nearly all the classics and standard books of literature, and age and grade was never considered in Father's method of educating his children. We had only one goal to aim for: college, and all the roads and bypaths of learning would lead us there if we desired that goal.

Almost every one of the New Jerseyites would act as teacher in our "play school" at intervals when Father and Mother were too busy to play. This added great zest and enthusiasm to our educational play, and it never became real work.

## Abram Berry and His Friends from Boyhood

Lyman N. Gary and Edward C. Harvey both stayed at the hotel for long periods of time. They were father's closest friends, from his school from boyhood days, and naturally, they took a sort of relative interest in Maple and me. They were Uncle Lyman and Uncle Ed to us.

Mr. Gary was a civil engineer, and this stood him in good stead as he personally surveyed all the land that he owned and sold through Morton and Stark counties. He had come west long before we had around 1882. He owned the town site and laid out the town of Taylor, and he named it for *David R. Taylor,* first Northern

Pacific Railroad superintendent, who lived in Mandan. Mr. Gary was a man of refinement and high ideals, and he did more than any man in the West at that time to promote the ethical standard of citizenship in Mandan and all the town sites that he surveyed and laid out: Mott, Flasher, Elgin, and the thriving south-line communities.

Mr. Harvey was a college man and held the position of land agent for the Northern Pacific Railroad Company, handling land grants from Bismarck to the Montana line. He traveled a great deal on the railroad and made his headquarters at Taylor. He had a claim of 160 acres adjoining the south boundary line of town. Harvey complied with all of Uncle Sam's laws to hold and own his homestead. He built a little two-by-four shack, dug a well, and put the land in cultivation with waving fields of golden grain. He slept in his little shack, in the lean-to with the single-pitched roof, but he had his dinners at noonday at the hotel. He did not sit at the table with the guests but would wait for our family table.

Harvey was such a likable person. His Eastern and Western experiences had broadened his mind and had developed in him that innate human sympathy that begets comradeship. He cemented to him the friendship of all with whom he came in contact.

Both Mr. Gary and Mr. Harvey were home-loving men, and as neither was married then, they enjoyed the society of our little family circle. When Maple and I would ask them to play teacher, they were always ready, and each would play the game in his own particular way.

Mr. Gary was serious-minded, and our "play school" had to bring forth worthwhile results, or he would not bother with us. When he played the role of "schoolmaster," we stood in awe of his severity and did not try any clowning. We studied diligently because we were ashamed to have him ask a question that we could not answer. He subscribed to the *Youth's Companion* and *Harper's Young People* for us, and sometimes our lessons would be from the reading matter in the magazines, or he would acquaint us with legendary or historical characters. The fanciful tales used by Socrates were as familiar to us as the Grimm's Fairy Tales.

It was quite different when Harvey assumed the role of "Professor Harvey." We never knew when he was serious and in earnest or when he was in a hoity-toity frame of mind. He would make a very severe face and call school to order with a band of his fist on the table. "Come to order, children!" He had several phrases that he would repeat, so we would listen eagerly for his opening words, such as: "Well, Well! The sea moaneth for the rest that never comes!" or "It's a rainy day here. children, but there's always sunshine somewhere in the world." He liked to have us recite verses and silly jingles, and this is one that he taught us:

"Little Miss Perkins,
Who loved pickled gherkins,
Went into the cupboard and stole some.
She then cried, "Alack!
My head's fit to crack;
I find them not very wholesome!"

One time I asked in all seriousness, "Professor, what makes thunder?"

"I am surprised that you ask!" he answered. "The angels in heaven play seesaw with a sheet-iron plank balanced on a cloud!"

This got a good laugh from us, and we thought it great fun to tell everyone who would listen. Harvey told us we could catch birds by putting salt on their tails, and one morning he walked in the hotel with a bird in one hand and the saltcellar in the other hand to prove this to us. He let the bird fly away and put the saltcellar back on the pantry shelf. His eyes twinkled with the enjoyment he got out of such play. One day he closed our school with this perplexing question: "What is it that has a mouth but never speaks and a bed but never sleeps?" We could not think of the answer, which was so easy and simple—a river. This one, "When does a lock get ripe enough to pick?" never seemed to have an answer, but it made us think. At other times he would be very serious and work with us over our mathematical problems and be very thorough with our geography to see that we knew the location of every country, city, town, mountain range, or lake we studied about.

Mr. Harvey was so very tall that he never knew what to do with his legs and feet, and when he sat in our low chairs he would stretch them across the room. He told us that he had "two-league boots," and it was just a few strides across the prairies to his "little old sod shack on the claim." Sometimes he would get a loaf of bread from Mother to take home for his breakfast. He would walk through the house to the office, stop and talk with Father and any others lounging around, and as he would chat with them, he would start nibbling on the loaf, picking out little bits from the inside. When he would leave for the shack, he would have only the empty outside crust of bread. With his long steps he was like a black streak across the prairie, and then, those watching from the hotel porch would see a light flash on in the one little window in the north wall of the shack. Mr. Harvey was home.

He had a subtle way of handling any obnoxious situation. One incident was when an uninvited guest moved into his shack in the stillness of the night. It was William Myers, the scapegrace of a wealthy old Mayflower family from Philadelphia. He was a manager but as irresponsible as a child with no sense of obligation and no object in life but to guzzle "old bourbon." Everyone called him Billy, and the diminutive fit his diminishing mental capabilities and his adolescent reasoning.

Billy was not a drunkard—never drank to the point of sobriety—but his one and only desire was to keep his system gloriously suffused with "spiritus lenis," as Father called it. He did not buy the cheap rotgut from the "blind pigs" but the genuine, bona fide "original package" allowed by the government for medicinal cure and dealing.

Billy's parents had coddled him for thirty-two years, and, tired of his playboy habits, they sent him to the great open spaces of the West, hoping that this would awaken him to a realization of life and its worthwhile opportunities. His allowance check came regularly, the first of every month, and this sufficed for a goodly supply of "tonic" if he economized on other necessities. This gave him the idea to "sponge" on all the Easterners on their claims, farms, and ranches.

Mr. Harvey came to Father and Mother with his problem. He said that Billy had been "booted" out of every place and had finally settled himself in his shack—fold-a-roll and baggage. He added, "Now don't be surprised, Abe, if Billy suddenly decides to change his abode! I've got to use some unusual diplomacy to get rid of that semisoused parasite! A gentle hint does not register in his sottish *[a drunkard]* brain!"

"I won't be surprised at anything," laughed Father, "and don't you be surprised if the hotel rooms are all occupied so that we cannot accommodate his highness!"

The next morning Mr. William Myers came in the hotel office, fuming and sputtering with disgust and distaste and "diseverything." He deposited his baggage: large Gladstone bag, plug-hat box, umbrella, and tennis racket on the floor and reached in his pocket for his bottle. He took a good deep-size swig and then paced the floor while he exploded in short stuttering sentences.

"I'm through! If the West can change a man to a hog, I don't want to live here! Ye gods, the dirty swine!"

"What's the excitement all about, Billy?" asked Father as he looked surprised.

"It's that damn Ed Harvey. You don't know the man, Berry. He's the personification of filth! Why, a man who can eat that way should live with filths!" Billy was pacing the floor, spitting into his handkerchief and wiping his mouth and raising his voice at Father. "Do you know, Berry, he's the dirtiest man I ever knew!"

"Why no, you don't mean Edward Harvey!" Father came right back to defend his friend. "I've known Ed since he was a boy. He's fastidiously clean! Clean in person, clean in habits and clean in mind! What more do you want in a man, Billy? What could he possibly do that's dirty?"

"His idea of economy is unadulterated filthiness! He made a rice pudding this morning, and what do you think he did? He put his dishwater in the stew pan to cook the rice! Now, can you think up anything dirtier than that? I've been there three months, and the Lord only knows what I've been eating. I'm so nauseated I'll never eat rice again; I'll always think of that dirty dishwater!"

Father put on the most perplexed, disgusted expression, overdoing it in an effort to keep from laughing at Harvey's adroit diplomacy.

Billy left on the next eastbound train for Mandan, where he could borrow enough money on his father's account to get back to his home in Philadelphia. His last words were, "I'm through with the West if it makes hogs out of men, and I'm through with the West and North Dakota."

## Letter Writing and Penmanship

Letter writing was a big feature of our education. Maple and I seemed to have started writing letters to Grandma Berry as soon as we could make marks with a pencil. Our letters grew until they became quite lengthy epistles of chronological data of the important events of our times. Father impressed upon us that a letter must carry some message worthwhile from the sender to the receiver, or it was not of a two-cent postage stamp value. His rules for good letter writing were:

"Don't say, 'I am well!' or 'Everyone is well.' Take that for granted. Don't speak about yourself or anyone being sick, unless it is really very serious. You should be ashamed to be sick because you admit that you don't know how to live or take care of yourself! Don't talk about the weather unless it is a hurricane, a cyclone, or an earthquake. All other weather is good weather; we don't want monotony, even in weather. Rain and wind are just as necessary to our well-being as sunshine.

"Write about the vital, interesting things that you do and that others are doing around you. Write about your home life and your pets. Write about the unusual things of the West. Write all the good thoughts that come in your mind. Imagine that person is with you, and you are telling them just what they would like to know. Then your letters will be worth a two-cent stamp!"

Father had absolutely forbidden Lyman Gary and Edward Harvey to teach us penmanship. He said, "Neither of you can write a legible hand. When I get your unintelligible scribbles I have to go to Dickinson to get a lawyer to decipher your Egyptian hieroglyphics! The saints forbid that my children should ever learn to write like that!"

We learned to write from Spenserian copy: books with clear, wide-open letters in freehand curves and flourishes. Our letters were like little storybooks covering every incident of our rapidly moving Western life. (Thanks to those letters now, they are helping me revive the memory of happy childhood days in the lengthened lands.)

Everyone we came in contact with we considered our teacher. We were eager to learn, eager to grow up, eager to walk out of the play school and into the great school of life, but we had never exerted ourselves in any study.

Our chance to walk out of the "play school" came sooner than we expected. Father overheard our schoolroom chatter. I said to Maple, "That arithmetic is a nasty little book! It makes the whole day miserable when I try to study it! I can add, subtract, multiply, and divide well enough, and I never use fractions if I can help it!'

## School Days in Taylor

When I get to be a grownup young lady I'll learn what I need, but I never want any more than I have to have of old mathematics."

Such was my unreasonable reasoning, and Maple, also, was following a study course of least resistance, and she expounded on her theory: "I feel just the same about grammar! Who cares about nouns and pronouns and verbs and adverbs and predicates and adjectives? I feel mad at everything else when I study them! Something is always pertaining to this, or something is always pertaining to that! Well, they can just pertain themselves to death for all I care! When we're grown-up young ladies I'll always do your arithmetic for you, and you can always tell me what is what with my grammar!"

Father suddenly appeared, and his face looked black as he bellowed at us, "So that is the way you study at 'play school!' You are cheating on your hard subjects! Now I'm going to find a female governor to settle the hash of you two little dummykins! I'm going to send you to college someday, and you're going to shame me with a half-rudimental education! No, you won't! You're going to study!"

With Father, action always followed thought. There was only one person available in Taylor to give home instruction. That was Mary Sloan, a footloose, carefree young woman of marriage age but unmarried, so she was unmistakably an "old maid."

Jonathan and Mary Sloan were from the northern part of New York State. They were both well educated and came from thrifty, honest, but close-fisted Scotch Presbyterian ancestry, which even the free Western spirit could not change.

Jonathan filed on a claim about thirty miles north of Taylor and started a cattle ranch. Mary took one of the choice claims that bounded the eastern borderline of town, built a comfortable little home, and planned on holding her claim and teaching in Stark County.

Father made an arrangement with Mary Sloan to take complete charge of our education; we could go to the town school when possible, study at home and keep abreast with the State school curriculum, but study, we must, and no more play with the subjects we loved the best.

Mary Sloan was old-fashioned and drably plain in her appearance. She was inclined more to mannishness than to femininity and even had a few mustachioed hairs in each corner of her mouth (which gave her a severe look), and her face rarely broke into a smile. None of the feminine frill and furbelows of that period adorned her person, and as for powder and paint, well, she was shocked and disgusted when she saw anyone who used it. She would say, "They are deceptions of the devil!"

At first she disrupted our happy, even-tempered household, and she made us antagonistic to what she tried to each, and Father tried to keep the tenor smooth. He said, "I know our home life seems higgledy-piggledy now, but we must adjust ourselves to this. Miss Sloan has the best education of any woman west of the Missouri River. We must be nice to her, or you won't be half educated!"

Nothing was funny; nothing was amusing to Mary Sloan. Father was a godless man who was bringing up his children in an unchristian atmosphere. She pitied Mother because she was married to such a hapless man. Her opinions did not come to us outright, but they would leak out to us in the classroom, and this would arouse our fire and indignation until we would rise up in a fighting mood or else rush out of the door, vowing never to return to her classes.

Miss Sloan was very meek and suppliant then, and we would go back to classes and try to be kind for Mother's sake. Religion was our most fertile ground of contention. Mary Sloan brought her own particular brand with her, and it was strictly to the letter of the Bible. She was straitlaced and autocratic in everything she taught.

School was always called to order with a prayer. We would kneel down by our chairs and bow our heads while she would offer a most suppliant plea for forgiveness for our sins. Maple and I would question each other: "She must be the sinner because we don't sin."

Her prayers would run on and on like this: "Dear Lord, as we kneel at thy feet we beseech thee to forgive us our sins. Forgive us as thou hast forgiven the pharisees, and lead us into the promise land! Oh, Lord, we beseech thee to keep us in the straight and narrow path for thy name's sake. Amen!"

This was only a hotchpotch of words to us and meant less. We had never been taught that we were sinners, but we would both come out with a very loud, "Amen!" We were in a prayerful position, but our minds were usually thinking of excuses to give to God. Surely He was too busy running the entire world and all the planets to stop and listen to this "gimble-gamble prayer."

I would say, "Please God, excuse her!"

While our heads were bowed, we would look across at each other and then at the bent and unattractive form of Miss Sloan. The soles of her number-eight house brogans would be standing on end, and her feet would be moving back and forth, giving force and emphasis to the words of her prayer. We would suppress our giggles but talk to each other by signs. Those waving soles were inviting to our "funny streak," and one day we gave in and chalked on them "POST NO BILLS."

She discovered this when she was at home and came back furious. Father tried to laugh it off and say that it was just "innocent fun." He had done the same trick when he was a boy in boarding school, so he blamed himself for the idea. We apologized on Father's excuse, and all was peaceful in the schoolroom again. Father then warned us, "Miss Sloan hasn't even got a 'funny bone,' so don't try any more tricks on her."

Our next flare-up came when Miss Sloan decided to teach us some religion as we were so sadly neglected at home. Heaven was her theme and did she ever lay it on! She built up a magnificent picture of golden streets and the throne room where the angels played golden harps while God and Jesus reigned supreme. Only the good could enter there, and she seemed to know who the good were in our community—as if God had let her in on His checkup.

All those who steal, drink, and swear cannot enter the kingdom of heaven. A lie, even a little white lie, would bar one from the gates. Not only one's actions but one's thoughts would put him or her in the bad place where he or she would burn in fire and brimstone. She read from the Bible and laid great stress and emphasis on her words, but our reactions did not please her. Then she laid down her Bible and looked at us, questioning: "Have you never been taught about the hereafter—about heaven and hell?"

Maple replied, her face happily serene, "Oh yes, we've heard that, but it doesn't bother us. We're not sinners, Father says."

Then I chipped in, "Father says that some people live in hell all the time, and they make the hell for themselves! He says that we are going to live in heaven now, and we'll keep right on living in the kind of heaven we like. We don't like harp playing. Father doesn't, and I never heard a harp. We've got a special heaven, and Father says it won't be crowded with hypocrites either!"

The argument got strong then. We knew that all the men around us, even those from New Jersey, swore (and we thought *damn* and *hell* were swearing), but we could not think that a just God would hold that against them for eternity. If God turned our best friends down, why, we best not have any use for such a God.

And then I spoke my mind: "If God is like you say, why He must be an old snoop, and I don't ever want to go inside of his old heaven! And I don't want anybody I love to go there either, so there!"

With that I grabbed my book and flaunted out of the room as Maple was saying, "You came here to help us with our arithmetic and our grammar! This is a day school, not a Sunday school!" And she flaunted out.

## School Days in Taylor

This took some explaining. Father and Mother heard our story, and then they had a long talk with Mary Sloan. The result was that she was not so worried over our religious views, and we accepted her whims and settled down to study. We curbed our tongues when she sent any barbed darts at our parents, our friends, the hotel, and the people who frequented it. She was a necessary fixture, and she had her good points, which we found when we scratched under her bigoted creed.

Jonathan Sloan would pop up in Taylor quite often and would stay at his sister's home. He would frequent the hotel, lounging around in the office smoking a cigar and chatting to anyone who dropped in. He did not tie up with a very strong bond to Father because he was equally as penurious *[stingy]* as Mary, but in a man it was more noticeable. Their Scotch stinginess was the butt of many jokes by everyone who knew them.

The Easterners called him the "Gay Lothario" *[a seducer of women]*, and while he had a very retiring manner, he had a side glance to his eyes that never failed to take in every detail of a woman's face and figure.

The cowboys would say that Jonathan always knew when a new girl was in Taylor. He would be working on his ranch when suddenly his head would raise high, and he would sniff the south breezes like a bull bison *[a buffalo]* for a female bison, then he would make a stampede for the township line. Someone would make the remark, "Sloan's goin' to town; I guess the new teacher has arrived or some female in skirts."

Those who saw Jonathan in town would remark to each other, "Did some swishy petticoat get off the train today?" These remarks were usually right; Jonathan liked to have some attraction when he left the dull monotony of his ranch life.

When a new teacher would come to the hotel to board, it was Jonathan who helped to make her feel at home. He would visit the hotel at once and ask her to play the organ, and then he would hang low over the keys and turn the music, gazing into her eyes.

There wasn't a musical string in his larynx, but he had a way of bawling out in a talking voice that made a prolonged resonant sound like blowing through a comb. His favorite song was "From Greenland's Icy Mountains to England's Coral Strand," and he would throw his head back and let the sounds fall where they may!

Father had jokingly asked him, "Let's you and I sing a duet, Jonathan!"

And the quick reply was, "All right Abe, when you can strike my pitch!"

"Strike your pitch!" said Father, "why, the law of gravity would keep us from singing together!"

Father had explained to us, "Do you know what the matter was with Jonathan's singing voice?" Of course, we didn't. "His epiglottis is upside down, and his trachea is lopsided," and Father spoke as if he knew. "Mine is just the opposite!"

Jonathan never seemed to make any progress with his various courtships. His visits would stop as suddenly as they had started. The singing would go on, but he was back on the ranch, and the breezes kept the secret locked with the south winds.

Mary Sloan taught us to be choice with our words and always use the word that would express our idea to its fullest value. When her house caught fire and burned to the ground, it was not a fire, it was conflagration, and it was the worst conflagration *[a big destructive fire]* that the Taylorites had ever seen in all their born days.

Not very long before this, Mary Sloan had given us a lesson on "The Laws of Cause and Effect," and now, in this natural phenomenon, we had before us a perfect demonstration of this law. Mary did not waste anything, and her economy verged on hoarding more than saving. Not a thing that came within her possession was ever given or thrown away. It had to wear out completely before she would give it up. The fire was caused by spontaneous combustion. She had thrown rags, paper, and masses of old things in the coal shed, and after these few years of accumulation, they had oxidized with enough rapidity to engender heat and ignite the whole mass.

Mary was in the living room at the time and smelled smoke. When she discovered the smoldering fire in the coal shed, she quite lost her head and did not know which way to run; she was too far away to call help, and water had to be pumped. The pump was temperamental and would not always pump water unless primed with water.

In the meantime, the Taylorites saw the smoke—a black column rising to the sky and drifting away in clouds. It was the best day of the year to have a real conflagration as the town was humming with people: farmers, ranchers and their families, and many cowboys and herders on horseback. Some of them had been drinking, either rotgut or "original package" stuff, and were keyed up to the point of hilarity, and they craved a little excitement.

Jack Andrews, in from the Antelope Ranch near Halliday gave a look at the black shaft of smoke, mounted his mustang, and did a Paul Revere daylight ride through Taylor. He rode down Main Street, then across the railroad tracks and down the road to Front Street, and over the railroad tracks again to the north border of town. He stopped before each building and house and shouted "Mary Sloan's house is burning!"

As Jack was about "three sheets to the wind," he began to get a little woozy, and his tongue got thick, and he was shouting, "Mary Schloon's schlouse is schurning!" and finally he was just shouting, but no one could distinguish a word.

People would look out, and those who had not seen the smoke would say, "Holy cripes! Some damn fool has gone loco again!"

Soon the whole town knew about the fire, and those who could were making a beeline there to act as a volunteer fire department. They went in wagons, buggies, on horseback, and on foot and they carried pails and gunnysacks with them. There was an army of them, and they divided their numbers into two groups: one group to carry out the contents of the house and the other to pump the water and throw it on the flames. It was ideal in weather, time, and conditions for a good rousing fire. The flames leaped high and merrily, consuming everything within their grasp within the coal shed.

The first group was able to carry everything out, almost at one time. They threw things on the ground at a safe distance from the house, in topsy-turvy confusion. Even the stove and all the food from the pantry was tossed. Every piece of furniture and all the clothes from the closets and even the castaway rummage trash from the attic were saved and unbroken.

It only lasted a short time, and the house was burned to the ground. Mary was running around in circles like a jackrabbit dodging the dogs and crying over her loss. The firefighters were wiping the perspiration from their brows while they looked at the junk that they had risked their lives to save. Father said, "Aren't you the craziest galoots this side of the Rockies! Look what you've saved! We got to see Mary in this ancient trumpery again!"

Then someone got the bright idea: "Take Mary away, Berry; we'll sort out this stuff! It ain't too late yet!" Father brought Mary Sloan back to the hotel for Mother to comfort, and while Mother gave her a cup of tea and some sweet rusk *[raised bread]* and jam to quiet her jumping nerves, the firefighters had a nice little fire of their own making.

Those from out of town went back to Taylor, and they all agreed it was the best fire they had ever fought. Those who were interested in the garb of their townswomen looked over the antiquated, much-worn clothes that Mary Sloan had brought from her hometown in New York State.

Each garment was held up for inspection and voted upon, and the majority won. "Yes" was for the "burnt offering" pile, and "no" was for the salvage pile. Almost unanimously, every garment and article voted upon got a hearty and decided "yes" vote. There was the black redingote that had a red rusty look, the flounced taffeta dress that could stand alone, the old gray bombazine that she wore for grand occasions, and any number of calico and gingham dresses that were so faded that a bystander said, "They look like the last roses of a long ago summer." Into that "Yes" pile went any number of coats, designed by the same New York tailor, who definitely could not decide whether to fashion them for a man or a woman. After the dresses and coats were decided, the hats came next. This caused a great deal of hilarity, as nothing is funnier than an ancient hat.

Some man would put the hat on his head, and the votes would ring out: "Yes!" "Yes!" "To the Fire!" "To the blazes!" There was Mary's old handwoven wheat-straw cartwheel, her poke bonnet of natural leghorn, her black Milan toque that came down to her ears, the two heavily trimmed turbans that looked like two overturned fruit crates, and then came the gray derby with its low rounded crown. It drove the Taylorites to distraction when she wore it. They had wanted to jump on it; such a hat was a disgrace to the town. Now was their chance. The old gray derby was kicked and stomped upon by everyone who could get a chance, until it was kicked right into the fire. The "burnt offerings" pile went up in smoke and ashes.

Mary Sloan's conflagration was really a godsend to the town. Mary took her loss very hard; she never could understand why her entire items were burned when everything else in the house was saved, and no one ever enlightened her. Every citizen in Taylor rejoiced over it, and when they saw Mary appear in some new dresses, coats with feminine lines, and fresh modern hats, they were more than happy. With the insurance money, Mary built a more modern and more comfortable house, and the town grew rapidly in her direction.

To impart knowledge to others by lessons is a gift. Mary Sloan had this gift, and she made it a business measured by dollars. She was a "splendid success" in Stark County as a teacher and also reconstructed their public school system to a high efficient standard.

Her ten rules for teaching were:

1. Begin everything with prayer.
2. Do everything in order, following the course of nature.
3. One thing at a time.
4. Often repeat the same thing.
5. Learn one thing before going to another.
6. Uniformity in teaching, which may be comparative.
7. Give no rules before you have given the examples.
8. Teach a thing first and then the reason for it.
9. Teach without compulsion. Nothing should be learned by heart.
10. Let everything be taught by induction and experiment.

Her only fault was that she did not know how to make her pupils love her. Father said, "She is the only petticoat pedagogue *[teacher]* we have out here. She can compress so much intellectual pemmican *[concentrated food]* in the minds of children!"

*Chapter Eight -*

# Hotel Proprietor Becomes a Land Baron

One of the most magnificent conceptions connected with the whole history of the country and of humanity at that time was the gradual and inevitable diffusion of different nationalities populating the vast prairies of the West. Whatever state they settled in, that was their state—the best state in the Union, and they could prove it in any an argument.

North Dakota boosters would gather on the hotel porch and boast and brag of the great wealth of their state and vaunt of the rich material resources that were yet untouched. In the heart of every man and woman there was a desire, active or slumbering, to win a part of God's splendiferous planet, and here was the great opportunity. These vast acres of prairie land were now in use by farmers and ranchmen and rapidly growing in value. It was difficult for the Easterner to understand the Westerner's system of raising stock.

There were numberless droves of cattle and herds of sheep throughout the state that did not have a roof over their heads nor a cut spear of hay to feed them. This stock would live through the often horrific winters without any particular care bestowed upon them and rarely with a loss. The oldest and most experienced ranchers of the West laughed at the thought of providing shelter and hay, and yet, the most carefully tended and housed cattle and sheep of the Eastern plains thrived no better than these.

The grasses of this midwest region ripened and cured, standing, carrying their nutritious qualities throughout the winter and furnishing as good fodder for stock amid the snows as the carefully preserved hay of the Eastern states. In fact, the Western stock had the most nutrition and was the hardiest.

There is about the same difference between the "bunch grass" and the "buffalo grass" of the prairies and the timothy and the herd's grass of the East as there is between an evergreen and a deciduous tree. The one is good through all the seasons, while the other dies and decays when the sap ceases to flow upward.

While it is true that North Dakota is located near the northern boundary of the United States and has very high and very low extremes of temperature, it never averaged as cold as it did on the same parallel of latitude in Minnesota. The average, at that time, was twenty degrees below zero at Taylor.

When the group on the hotel porch would argue about the degrees of temperature in the East and the West, Jacob Wade, of Oxford, New Jersey, would say, "I swan if it isn't colder back in my lil ol' hometown than it is out here. I swan if it didn't go down to thirty degrees below zero every winter I lived in that blasted little ole town! That's only seventy-five miles west of New York City too! Every citizen in Oxford looks for chilblains, expects chilblains, and gets chilblains as soon as winter sets in, an' he never gets disappointed!"

In the dry clear atmosphere of the West one felt the cold far less at twenty below zero than in New Jersey at fifteen degrees less. As for chilblains, well, the Taylorites thought the least said about them the better, as they were very numerous but very unpopular when cold weather set in. It was not considered unmannerly to scratch your feet and hands in the lost polite society, and if one started the sport, the rest would soon follow suit by digging in to relieve their itching. Father would often come in from the office in an evening and say, "We've just had a chilblain party out there to see which one could outscratch the other."

In the autumn when the Easterners would gather on the porch, they would all start praising the sublime beauty of prairie scenery, then their minds would reminisce. Edward Harvey would say, "I have seen the Rocky Mountain magnificence, but there is something more peaceful and sublime in this prairie quietude."

Seb Morrison, the sheriff, would reflect in his slow drawl, "I have floated down the mighty Colorado River through its mountain gate and its wild canyons, seen its cataracts and resistless rapids, but give me the prairie's rolling symmetry!"

Lyman Cary would express his thoughts: "I have been filled with awe at the magnitude and majesty of the wonderful Cumberland Mountains, but I am filled with greater awe in the solitude of the prairies!"

Father would add his reflections: "I have climbed the Jersey Hills near Morristown and looked down upon the valleys and plains, the farmlands. I have stood in the lowlands and looked up at the Jersey Hills. I love them, boys. I grew up there, but the prairies have got me now—smooth and arable, waiting for cultivation! I'm going to have some of God's land, boys; I can see it now in the offering!"

When Father talked about owning a farm or a ranch, his listeners always treated his cravings as a joke, but Father was in earnest and was planning and acting to make his dreams come true.

The Easterners would tell him, "You're not built right for a rancher—too full in the girth!"

One would say, "You can't run a ranch from a swivel chair or from behind a high-top desk!"

Father would answer them, "Whatever I have will be run scientifically, and I'll need both the chair and the desk and a footstool for my feet. By the way, I'll need a 'double-entrance' ledger, a large blotter, and an ink eraser, if you don't mind!"

One day Father came home from Dickinson, overflowing with exuberance and infelt happiness. He walked in the living room where Mother, Maple, and I were and waved a paper wildly over his head.

"Here I am, carrying a nature full of feeling, and when a man is full of feeling, up to the very brim, he cannot carry himself without spilling over! Bow down, slaves! I'm a land baron! We must now toil to make the West like the East!"

Maple and I ran to him, put the palms of our hands to our foreheads, and made deep salaams, prostrating ourselves on the floor at his feet. I said, "Abdul Abraham, what news bringest thou?"

While Maple did a lot of jibberish and deep bowing, Mother said, "Stop being so silly, and let's hear the news from Farmer Slow."

## Contract with Uncle Sam

Father waved the paper and handed it to Mother. "This is my contract with Uncle Sam. He gives me 160 acres of free land if I plant and cultivate five acres into a forest of trees!" Father carried out his part of the contract and planted five acres on land that had never grown anything but clumps of high, tough buffalo grass. He planted them with sturdy little cottonwood trees, which are a hardy species of poplar.

The planting of those trees made a Taylor holiday, as all the New Jerseyites and all those who had a free day in town officiated at the making of the first Stark County forest. Father said that it would be the first forest; many others had tried but had not succeeded. Now he would prove that trees would grow on prairie land. He envisioned his little cottonwood saplings growing to great heights and making a shaded forest on this west plain like an oasis in a desert land.

Maple and I would make magic with our daydreams and call up a vision of a dense grove that would be cool and inviting so people would come from miles around to have picnics. We envisioned hammocks and swings suspended from the cottonwoods. All of the Jerseyites had visions as they helped to plant the trees.

Jonathan Sloan would stop at his task many times to swallow the lump in his throat and dream out loud. "I hope this will give us a touch of red and yellow in the fall, Berry." Then he would swallow again, "But it won't take the place of the flaming maples or the golden elms (gulp) or the scarlet ash trees (gulp) or my old York State hills" (gulp)! No one laughed at Jonathan then.

Edward Harvey envisioned its beauty: "We are going to make the earth grow splendid out here! We'll add to this picturesque scenery!"

Father would stand at the highest elevation and look over the undulating acres of waving buffalo grass, unbroken by even a rock. In the West was the rise of Young Man's Butte on the horizon to relieve the sameness of view. There was something majestic and grand in the prairie outline that was felt by all who gazed upon it.

Father would sing over and over, "I'm a land baron; I'm a land baron!" And then "I am lord of all I survey!"

Then Lyman would add, "Ah, but you didn't survey this, Berry; I did!"

Lyman Cary was always praising the salubrity of the northwestern part of the state. "This is the health route, and all roads lead you to it. There are no diseases lurking in this clear, pure ozone of the prairies! Those who are sick bring their diseases in from the outside. The valetudinarian *[person in poor health]* travels out here and finds it a haven for the mere recovery of spirits and the complete restoration of health!" It was true; salubrity was one of the eminent recommendatory qualities of this section. The new settlers boasted of it, and the old settlers bragged that they could not start a cemetery in Stark County until someone shot a man. They said that the young people did not die, and that the old people got a new lease on life and lived on.

I recall the first time Maple and I visited the cemetery. We were in the buggy with Father and Harvey, just riding around to give our horse, Smoky, some exercise when we came upon this fenced-in plot north of town. We all got out of the buggy, tied Smoky to the corner of the white picket fence, and walked around inside to look at the tombstones that marked the graves. There were not very many for the size of the grounds, but the land company gave the plot to the town site, and they were very generous with their broad outlook for the future.

The tombstones were very unusual: just slabs with rounded corners, hewn from hard Montana vitreous *[like glass]* quartz. They were shaded from colorless white and pink to deep purple and brownish yellow with veins of gold running through in zig-zag markings. Harvey was reading the names and seemed very surprised. "Well, I'll be damned! Most of these poor devils were shot!"

Berry said, "Yes, and all those in that corner were shot for rustling cattle or stealing horses, so the country is better off without them."

"Now look here! Those who didn't get shot committed suicide" said Harvey. Then we walked over to the far north corner where there was a caved-in grave, isolated by a fence of its own. The grave was completely covered with Russian thistles, piled high and thick and pressed down. We could hardly see the inscription on the flat stone: "Tathan Jorgenson, age 68 years."

"Poor old Tate!" said Father. "He was the wickedest cuss who ever breathed this pure unadulterated air! He hated everybody, and when he got so he hated himself, he wanted to die!"

"Is he the one who planned his own suicide and had his neighbors watching him?" asked Harvey. Maple and I had heard the story many times, but it was really hard for us to comprehend its awesomeness.

"He told everyone that he was going to kill himself, and then he invited two of his Norwegian neighbors in to watch him" he said. "They all filled up on a hot alcohol punch, and then he made his own bullet. He had hardly enough powder left, but he put all he had in that bullet. The two neighbors told just what happened!"

Father always went through the motions when he told the story. "Tate placed the muzzle of his pistol about a foot from his head and pulled the trigger with his thumb. He was such an awkward cuss. The boys said that the bullet crawled wearily out of the barrel, passed through that foot of space, and managed, by great exertion, to imbed itself in Tate's brains. The boys went home then and had a good sound sleep, and the next day they came to Taylor and told the news."

We walked away from the grave then, and Berry continued: "They finally decided to bury him in that corner, but they couldn't get a funeral cortege *[ceremonial procession]*. Annie and I went, along with some of the women who felt sorry for him. I'll send a boy out here someday to take the tumbleweed off his grave. I do believe someone gathers them up and puts them inside the fence. The winds could never pack them in there so tightly!"

"Here is another suicide," said Maple. "I remember when he hanged himself, and he was the coroner in Dickinson." On his tombstone was this inscription: "Patrick Donnelly, Age 53, He lived and died a suicide." We stopped in front of two other graves, with headstones, sided by side: "Mike Flynn, age 54, and Bridget Flynn, age 52."

Father explained, "They ran the section house for a year. They say they both died from milk leg, but the way they staggered around, I think it was booze that got in their legs, not milk!" There were a few graves of the townspeople who had died before we came west; but our graveyard was not a very thriving place.

## A Bonanza Year

Father said that he remembered that all the speeches in New Jersey commenced with that old familiar sentence: "One hundred years ago, etc." But in North Dakota the speeches usually started with, "One year ago" or "Two years ago" but never longer than

"Seven years ago," and this always struck the ear with a welcomed freshness.

It was about this time that all the old settlers were harping on this phrase: "Seven years ago we had a bonanza year!" and then an old-time farmer named Sid would profess, "Mark my word: this year we are due for a bonanza humdinger in any crop we plant!"

Sid was the court's professional prophesier. Several years ago he had a mishap while on a roundup in the Killdeer Mountains. He was well mounted on a trained mustang, but in cutting out the steer from the herd, the pony made a quick swerve that threw Sid down an embankment, with the pony on top of him. Everything came out all right but Sid's leg, and as he expressed it, "I looked at that ole leg, and it was as flat as a flapjack! I never expected to use the damn thing again!" Then if anyone would listen, Sid would go into details about his recovery, riding into Fort Berthold, Indian reservation, on the same little mustang, where an Indian medicine man packed his leg in mud and herbs until it was restored to normalcy again. His leg was crooked and about two inches shorter than the other one, but it was a leg, and it turned Sid into a human barometer.

He would explain, "I can 'sensitate' the weather with my bashed-up leg." And Sid was usually right. This year Sid said that his leg did not have any twinges of pain; in fact, it was as normal as the other leg, so that was more than just fair-weather forecasting. "Yep, I ain't been a weather prospect for nothin'! This here leg is actins' jus' like a decent leg, so that means something' good! I'm a tellin' you: this is a bonanza year!"

Sid had made so many true prophecies that everyone believed him. The phrase began to travel around the countryside, and men, women, and children echoed it: "We are due for a bonanza crop!" "A seven-year bonanza!"

The "cracker-box brigade" talked it over in the General Store instead of lying down and telling how the government in

Washington should be run to help the West. The "tobacco-spitting contesters" gave their unbiased opinion as they sat in the post office waiting for the mail to be sorted out. They would chew tobacco and spit, with a long directed aim at the sawdust box in the middle of the room. They kept score of the "spitter" because those who missed had a treat to pay for later. They agreed unanimously that a bumper crop was due. Crops ran in cycles in these prairie states. We had just had seven years of just fair cribs, so we were due for a bumper. This was their only topic of conversation; local politics had rusted out and even prohibition had lost its fervor *[warmth of emotion]*. No new controversies had arisen to stir up arguments and debates.

Farmers were plowing and cultivating their entire land acreage. Stock raisers turned some of their timothy and alfalfa fields into wheat fields. Many farmers mortgaged their property and pledged the shirts off their backs to procure money to buy seed wheat or to rent more land for their extensive cultivation.

A touch of the bonanza fever got in Berry's veins because he had the remaining acres of his tree-claim plowed and sowed with number-one Hard Durham Wheat. He also turned the few acres he owned near the hotel into a wheat field. He said, "If this state is really due for a bumper crop, I want to be in on the harvest!" Then he would sing that old hymn in his off-key, untuneful voice: "What shall the harvest be, be, be; what shall the harvest be?"

Dave Riggleman from Mott kept a diary of crops, and with this he could prove that North Dakota was blessed by providence with a seven-year plan. He was in Taylor buying seed wheat and talking to the Taylorites: "I kicked myself all around the claim, the 160 acres, and seven years ago for just planting the usual acreage. I'll never be caught again with my planting unreckoned!"

During the spring and summer all the elements of nature seemed to working together in harmonious rhythm: rain and sunshine, sunshine and rain, with regularity and abundance. Never during the season did the ground lay scorched and dry. Never during the season did the rainfall come too heavy or too persistent. The farmers could hardly sleep at night. They put in tense and anxious days and nights as the season wore on, and they were depending entirely upon the elements.

Wind clouds would gather, threatening to send a tornado or a cyclone over the lengthened lands. Then, it was as if a magic hand would appear: the clouds would be brushed rudely and quickly away to move down the Missouri Slope trail to lose their volume and velocity in the upper stratus of air.

As the season moved on with everything looking more and more favorable for a bonanza crop, the citizens began to get out their lead pencils, even to the little old stubs, and use any piece of paper that they could find. Groups would congregate in town and figure on the walls of buildings, inside and outside. They would figure on the fences and even on the hitching posts. One could overhear their conversations:

"I can't believe it! Sixty million…seventy million! Why, they're crazy!" "Gee-hoss-a-fat! It can never be! Seventy-five million bushels at eighty-five cents a bushel—or maybe ninety-five! Gee-hoss-a-fat!" "Gee-willikins! There are four hundred people in this blasted little old state—and with one hundred seventy-five million dollars to be divided among us! We'll all be rich! Gee-willikins!"

Thor Thorgenson wore his pencil out—lead and rubber figgerin' on his one-hundred-acre crop. "At thirty bushel to the acre and 'spose I get one dollar an even bushel—maybe! I'll buy myself a plush sof'fee and sit in it the rest o' my natural life!"

Bill Young from Flasher, Morton County, was simply astounded at the showing his first crop made. He formerly lived in Newton County, Indiana, and he liked to make comparisons. "I've got wheat, oats, and flax, and it's the mightiest good-looking crop I ever saw. My wheat heads are eighteen inches long. Some folks object to being so far from the railroad as I live, but pshaw! I'd rather live forty miles from town and have something to take in to sell than live in town and have nothing. It's the truth!"

The month of August arrived, and the spirit of prophecy hardly dared describe the fulfillment thereof. The wheat fields had reached their matured abundance. The tall stalks were bowed with the heaviness of the bearded spike of flowering spikelets, and each wheat grain was plumped to fatness. The outcome of the crop was beyond all dreams and all visions—and even beyond all the stub-pencil figuring of the farmers and claim settlers.

Active must be the ardent imagination that can see the beauty and sublimity of these vast acres of waving wheat with their life-sustaining power. One must envision himself or herself standing upon the crest of the world, with all this beneath his or her eyes, if that individual would comprehend the entire scene, from the Badlands on the Western border to the slopes of the Red River Valley on the Eastern line. That person would stand there, an enraptured spectator, and exclaim, "What a sublime panorama of golden glory."

The idea of such a picture can never be conveyed by words. It is a picture that must be painted by the wonder-working power of the paintbrush of ideality: the golden sunshine pouring down on ripened fields of golden grain and, in some places, extending from horizon line to horizon line. Sunshine, moisture, and "elbow grease" had wrought this bonanza crop—the seven-year wonder of North Dakota! Wheat had always been considered "the silent partner." Now, wheat had become the outspoken, loquacious partner, and it spoke so loudly that the farmer did not know which way to turn or what to answer. All the land was full of people—restless, struggling, toiling, and striving.

As competition is always considered the life of business and trade, so every milling company was conveying with the other to get the most business. Elevators were springing up overnight at every convenient shipping point, and large signs read, "We buy wheat, and we welcome your patronage!"

If the farmers went "haywire" while the wheat was growing, they went "double haywire" when the harvest was ready. Every farmer in the bonanza area had "loco disease" in one of its stages, according to the acreage of his crop. Wheat was affecting the people just like the loco weed and producing very much the same symptoms in everyone who had a crop ready for the harvest. This "loco disease" was a sort of brain delirium, a vision of richness that overwhelmed its victims with the realization of abundance. These farmers desired to express themselves in some manner of indulgence, a splurge of inflation, an effervescence *[to bubble over]* of their own infelt greatness.

When one would see the "bosses and "overseers" of the large wheat farms driving around the country in shiny new red buggies with matched-up horses, and a Mail-Order Harness, and wearing kid gloves on their calloused hands, he would feel the urge to laugh long and loud.

Maple and I wanted to laugh when we saw this, but Father put his two first fingers to his lips and stifled his outburst of merriment and said: "Don't you dare laugh, you little simplekins! I'm going to buy myself an outfit that will beat that! I'm going to buy a tooled-carved leather saddle and gloves to match, with wristlets! Tee-hee!" We controlled ourselves to hear: "I'm going to buy Mother a pair of ceremonial white kid gloves, elbow length. She wanted them when we lived in New Jersey, and I didn't buy them for her. I'll be darned if she won't get them now." We laughed again, and he added, "As for you two little darlings, I'll import a French teacher right from Paris, and you'll study! I'll buy two little straightjackets studded with...with...studs!"

"No, you don't," Maple said. "We are going to have a little bit of loco weed ourselves! Dottie wants a red coat trimmed with succotash braid, and I want a parasol with ruffles."

## Harvesting Crews and Threshing Machines

Now the time had come for the gathering and garnering of this bonanza wheat crop, which nature had so bountifully bestowed upon the North Dakotins. The fits of "loco" would come and go, but the wheat was ripe, and action must be backed by sanity.

The prairie landscape changed overnight. Harvesting crews were in the fields, ready to take over. There was work for everyone, and every man had his own particular job. Men came in from other states, even from Canada, and some from the Mexico border. Women and children had their part to play in the bonanza harvest, and even the hobo, the "knight of the railroad track" could find work if he craved it.

First upon the scene were the reapers. Indeed, proud was the man who sat upon the high seat, holding rein over four horses while he guided the machine around and around the wheat field, cutting wide swaths of the sun-ripened wheat. The reaper worked with its great revolving fans that swept the grain stalks close to the shuttling knives and then the little device that worked like a pair of human hands, tying the sheaves in even bundles to be tossed off the receiving rack onto the stubble field. Ah, man's clever ingenuity was continually working to save labor!

For fields of larger acreage there was another type of reaper, with a shaft attached that would carry the sheaves up a chuteway and drop them into a double-bodied farm wagon that would follow by the side of the reaper. They were then taken directly to the threshing machine, saving an extra handling.

The women and children worked in the fields placing the sheaves in upright stacks. I have a happy recollection of Maple and I helping Father gather the sheaves when the reaper swathed through the grain acres of our tree claim. We picked each sheaf up carefully so as not to let the grain rattle out. Two sheaves must stand up and hold each other up, "like two drunken men." Around these two sheaves we would pack eight or nine and then pass on to make another stack. Father had most of his "satellites" from the hotel with him, and we made it a sort of gala day, where work was play, and we all had fun. He would march around singing the old hymn, "Bringing in the sheaves, bringing in the sheaves; here we come rejoicing, bringing in the sheaves." All the others would join in, and soon we could not hear Father's out-of-tune crescendo. A picnic lunch would be the climax of this play-working day, and before anyone could get tired, we would be back at the hotel, "for a bonanza rest," Father said.

The threshing machines were the most important and the greatest attraction of the harvest season. They were like living things, land serpents with long red bodies, crawling along the roads and settling down in the middle of a stubble field. Like the prehistoric animals that they resembled, they had ravenous appetites and would devour the grain, sheaf by sheaf, and belch with every mouthful. Their breathing and snorting could be heard for miles away: a long drawn=out "chug-a-de-chug-chug, chug-a-de-chug-chug" and then another sound like "riddle-de-de, riddle-de-dum, riddle-de-de, riddle-de-dum" as the big fan belt rolled around. The breadth of this land monster would come out in dense black smoke and rise in a straight column to lose itself in the vastness of the blue overhead canopy. It would not even darken the whiteness of the windless clouds.

The kid-glove farmers and overseers would ride around to listen to this musical cadence of the threshing machine in their own fields, and it was sweet to their ears. The harvest picture was vivid and beautiful for those who could see it without counting their money. The bright vermillion-red of the threshing machine contrasting with the golden-yellow of the ripened wheat, while overhead, the sun would ride majestically through the clear blue of the heavens and pour its beams direct, like molten gold over the cultivated acres of the lengthened lands.

For this bonanza crop, threshing machines of every type and construction were called into action. The latest and most improved form was the "agitator" with all its labor-saving devices. This machine had attained a very high operative perfection with an immense capacity for threshing and cleaning wheat ready for the market. These largest of machines threshed over four thousand bushels of wheat under favorable conditions and were driven by an engine of fifteen to twenty horsepower. Into its great mouth the automatic feeder would push the unthreshed sheaves, while a little gadget would cut the string band that held them. As the sheaves would pass through the machine, the wheat, straw *[hollow stalks]* and chaff *[husks of grain]* were separated; the wheat was cleaned, weighed, and sacked.

The straw was automatically blown out through a long upright shaft with a hood on the end to guide the straw into the stack. This Netherlander blower-stacker was the "last straw" invention, as it would make a much larger and better stack of straw than could be made by man, acting as pitchers and levelers. There were many of the old-style threshing machines of the "vibrator" class, operating throughout the state. They were used on the smaller farms and were more easily moved from place to place.

The "newfangled" threshing machines brought out the tourists and sightseers from East, West, North, and South. The bonanza crop was a self-advertisement for the West. It was now indeed "The Golden West!"

The land agents were as thick as flies around sorghum *[cereal]* grass grown for grain, syrup, and fodder. They would bring prospective land buyers to see the threshing operation, and if no one had a chance to "put a bug in their ear," the prospective land buyers thought that every year brought such a crop to North Dakota.

Abram and Annie Berry – Their Team – Baxter and Bixby – 1895 on A-BAR-B Ranch

The roadways were hardly left free long enough to lay the dust. Every type of conveyance was bringing the people to see the "threshing show." There were buggies, buckboards, carry-alls, surreys, and even lumber wagons with rows of seats. Some came on bicycles, and a few horseless carriages would venture over those two-track, high-in-the-middle roads. Sometimes these "gasoline buggies" had to be towed back by a team of horses, and then there would be much laughter and hilarity as the farmers would yell, "Get a horse! Get a horse!" Maple and I loved riding our horses through the prairies; the wind didn't bother us because we wore our hair in pigtails. We ran errands for Father and Mother as well as helped with the sheaves.

Threshing was a whirlwind job all over the country. Wheat was standing full and ripe and threshing machines were traveling from one farm to another. There was a western phrase, "I am hungry; I can eat as much as a thresher." That meant to the utmost stretch of one's capacity, and that would have shamed a gourmet at

## Hotel Proprietor Becomes a Land Baron

an eating contest. It took fuel to keep the threshing engine going, and the thresher's body engine had equally as hard a task.

This was the time when the farm women showed off the epicurean masterpieces of their culinary art. Food of every description—homegrown and home prepared, wholesome, nutritive, and digestible—graced the harvester's table. It was more sumptuous than a banquet feast in New Jersey or ritzy New York, according to our Eastern settlers.

The secret of this good cooking was in the judicious use of fresh eggs, milk, and homemade butter. There was crusty brown bread from unprocessed flour, roasts of pork, beef, mutton, or poultry done to perfection, juicy and tender. Milk gravy was poured over mashed potatoes, and the dessert would be slabs of pie. Fruit did not grow very plentiful in North Dakota, so pies were mostly lemon cream, custard, and molasses. There were glorified bread puddings and tapioca cream puddings, and coffee was served all through the meal. The stimulating aroma of freshly ground Arbuckle's coffee tickled the nose nerves of the hungry men, tempting them to drink to the third and fourth cup. The table usages of polite society were not known among a threshing crew or, if known, were not heeded.

Biceps Joe was the "A Number One" thresher of the stacking crew. When he sat down to a table, he would say, "Now, every fool for himself, and the devil help us all." He had the muscle, but Milton Schlosser, the straw boss, had the longest reach. That meant the full length of his arm and down his long lean torso to where he bent to sit down. With the slant to his legs, he could reach any food within six feet of his plate, and woe to him who tried to grab the dish he was after!

Sam Braman sat at the head of his table when they came to his ranch. His ranch was second to Milton's. When he would stretch five and three-fourths feet over the table, his wife, Lou, would yell from the kitchen, "Sit down! Where's y'ur ed-ti-cat, Sam?"

And he would reply, "Ate it, an' I want sum more." One time he answered, "I ate it, but I didn't know it was cat."

Lou came in and jerked him back in his seat and smacked him as if he was a baby. "Now sit where you're set!"

All was in good fun, and there was much laughing and bantering over the "threshing tables." They all felt rich and would ask the other, "What are you going to do with all your spoliation *[over-indulgence]*?" When pretty girls, young matrons and even plain vivacious young things were waiting on the tables, there would be flirting, winking, and understanding byplays going on all around that the most ravenous, vociferous *[noisy]* eaters did not notice or comprehend. While most of the threshers were noisily concentrated on "feeding their innards," Dan Cupid, that ingenious little Roman god of love, would cleverly contrive to further his romance business.

North Dakota's prettiest girls, with rose-flushed faces, the fairest blooms of every nationality, would flutter around the tables like bright butterflies. They would wait on everyone, pouring coffee, filling and passing dishes, but particularly would they wait on the suntanned, brawny youths from other states. Some of these farmer boys brought their home manners with them and did not reach and sprawl over the table but asked for things with a polite, "Please, ma'am." Hands would touch hands, eyes would meet eyes, and eyes would wink, and glances would tell far more than the spoken word what heart said to heart and soul to soul. These age-old messages of love would send their magnetic currents flashing around the long tables, and no one else was the wiser, not even an all-knowing mother.

Sly little Dan Cupid got in his best licks in the long evening twilight when the threshing machine was silent and most of the overly tired workers had already "hit the hay" to recuperate for the next day before them. New love would saunter out for a stroll along the roadways by the stubble field or to a bench under the cottonwoods.

*Hotel Proprietor Becomes a Land Baron*

The same old moon that had peeked at lovers through forests, hills, and valleys would envelope the prairie landscape in a sheen of misty loveliness. There was a subtle gaiety in the grandeur of the prairies at night, enchanted by the luxurious variety of cloud shadows that brought young lovers close in spirit and akin to nature.

This was not idle lovemaking for pastime but sincerity of heart with a keen desire to take part in this great action game of life. For them it meant a deep joy in the mere living for a purpose. To these prairie sweethearts, love meant a home of their own; it meant acres and acres of God's earth to till and make productive, and most of all, it meant the blessing of little toddlers to make new tracks in the prairie's sod. Dan Cupid worked these same tricks, and many more, on the North Dakota boys. He aimed true and pinioned their hearts with out-of-state girls who had come across the line to help with the harvest of the seven-year bumper crop. That was also a bumper year for the marriage-license bureau.

The hotel was very busy these days, keeping pace with all the people who were coming and going. Money was flying around like "winged victory." Mother had extra girls to help her. The dining room could no longer have a cozy corner; it was every inch an eating room. The bedrooms were doing double duty, with cots added and extra beds arranged wherever space would allow. Mother's home-cooked meals kept up their high standard, and Mother would smile and explain when the guests would praise her, "I only know one way to cook, and that is just as I cook for my family! I always teach my help to cook the same way. We like to have everyone feel that this is their home!"

Mother had to help in the hotel office now as Father was rushing here to there and everywhere. He said, "I've got all my irons in the fire, and they're all red hot at once." The warehouse took up most of his time; it had been enlarged to take care of this surplus wheat. It was remarked that even the grains of wheat were larger and plumper and quite outdid themselves in growing for this bonanza year. Wheat, wheat, wheat! No—number-one Hard Durham Wheat. It was coming into Taylor on every main road and every byroad, from north, east, south, and west. In every direction one looked, there could be seen long lines of double-bodied lumber wagons filled with sacks of wheat and drawn by two or four horses. Some of the heaviest loads were drawn by ox teams. Those patient animals were all pulling with their heads bowed and their traces taut, but the roads were level and soft under hoof.

Wheat, wheat, wheat! The same high-grade "A Number One" wheat was going out of Taylor in double-tiered, binned-up freight cars, long trainloads at a time. This wheat was going to the grain mills in Mandan, Minneapolis, St. Paul, and St. Louis to be ground into the best flour in the world and to be shipped around the world.

Representatives of every mill were buying wheat in Taylor. Father was buying for the Mandan Roller Mills Company and getting his full share. He made no effort to outbid or out buy anyone. The warehouse was working to its fullest capacity, and there was a large sign in red lettering on the front that read: "Bring Your Grain to Us as Soon As it is Threshed, The Money's Ready - The Price - The Markets Best." Father would attend to the weighing, grading, and buying of the wheat himself.

He would stand in the doorway while the wagon loads would draw up in front on the platform scales. I can see him now with his long white Ulster, his wide-brimmed Stetson hat pushed back on his head, and a pencil tucked over his ear. Wherever Father was, there was jolly laughter and a well=satisfied feeling as the farmer would receive the money for the bumper crop.

The biggest bonanza farmers were paid in checks, and the checks ran into the thousands. The number-one bonanza farmer received his check for $25,000, and that was the check that changed the whole town of Taylor. There were several No. 2 bonanza farmers who received the sum total each of $15,000, and there were innumerable bonanza farmers who cashed in their crops for $10,000 more or less.

The rest of the bonanza farmers thought that they were rich with anything around $5,000, according to their acreage. The small claim rustlers wanted to see the color of their money, so Father paid them in cash with "yellow boys" and silver "cartwheels." Money came easy that bonanza year, and it changed hands rapidly. These who went "loco" enjoyed it to the utmost. The majority of the citizens were of the staid *[temperate]*, home-loving folk of every nationality, and they were level-headed and with broad visions. Their future and the education and future of their children were at stake—money spent wisely.

*Chapter Nine -*
# Round House Engine – Ol' Brute

About the only thing in Taylor at that time that was complaining was the round-house engine, "Ol' Brute." This was the locomotive that had the job of scuttling the freight cars around on the side tracks. It had to scuttle an empty car in back of the warehouse to be filled with wheat, and when it was filled, it had to scuttle the car onto the main side track where the outgoing train was formed. Ol' Brute was like a human personage, like a man who had a good job but didn't appreciate it and would complain about it all the time. When it was pushing or pulling an empty car into position, it would sputter and spout black smoke and sometimes refuse to budge.

It was Abram Berry who named the old engine, and he would interpret the growling, grumbling, and fault-finding sounds it made. "Chug-chug-chug-a-dee-chug-chug!" said "I don't want to do it." "Puff-puff-a-dee-puff-puff" meant "I won't do it again!" Then Ol' Brute would fume and fuss to get the loaded car away from the warehouse and attach it to the train. By this time it would be so exasperated that it was actually swearing in blue-smoke cuss words: "Puff-i-ty-puff-f-f." "Well, I'll be damned! And "Toom, Toom…too…toom!" was "Damn it to hell."

That performance went on every day, and the whole town knew Ol' Brute and his bad temper. The engineer, Tom Toyne would say in a jovial way, "Yep, Ol' Brute is in a great peeve today! He is swearing he'll stop on me, but I'll break his ol' iron heart if he doesn't get these wheat cars a movin'!"

Maple and I would watch Ol' Brute for hours, scuttling on the side tracks. We would try to think up new phrases for its human-like grumbling, but it always said the words that Father gave to it.

When the wheat cars were in readiness, a large, extra-horsepower locomotive would "choo-choo" right on the scene. This engine did not complain like Ol' Brute but was very determined and businesslike, and with bold decision, it would move the heavy train onto the main track. With rhythm, "Chug-chug-dee-chuggity-chug" it traveled northeastward around the bend of the road, on past Young Man's Butte, out of sight over the horizon, and its black column of smoke would vanish in the blue distance.

The Taylorites would cheer as their wheat went on its way to the mills. They would wave their hats and throw them into the air and sing,

> The train is going around the bend;
> Good-bye, my lover, good-bye.
> There goes my wheat around the bend;
> I have the money to lend and spend;
> Good-bye, my lover, good-bye;
> My lover, good-bye, good-bye!

One day when everyone in town was watching the wheat train going around the bend, cheering and singing lustily, the column of smoke did not vanish. It grew denser and blacker, and then, a line of red would shoot up with the smoke. This told us plainly that the prairie was on fire. A live coal spark from the engine of the wheat train had ignited the dry buffalo grass that grew rank and tall on the track bed. The fire was traveling rapidly over this flammable tinder. The cheering and singing changed suddenly to the fire call—a long shrill whistle blew and blew.

Every mother's son, every "blasted, blooming hombre" in town was in action and off to the fire. They went in every conveyance handy and carried barrels of water, brooms, rakes, and a supply of gunnysacks to smother the flames. The nearby farmers hitched their horses to plows to turn over the sod for fire breaks.

## Round House Engine – Ol' Brute

Father was leaving the warehouse when he heard the commotion and saw the smoke. The wind was leading the fire toward his little grove of cottonwoods. He scooped up every firefighting thing available and jumped in a lumber wagon that was headed for the scene of action.

The fire had reached the tree claim, and the flames were like serpents with long tongues. They wrapped themselves around the tree trunks and reached out to every branch and twig. The jackrabbits scurried out of the underbrush but only ran a little way, as if they would be secure and protected in another part of the grove. Their intuition was right. The firefighters saved about one-third of the little grove.

Father said, "I cried when I saw the charred and blackened stumps of my brave little cottonwoods. They had withstood the frost and the winds for one year, and now, a fire was the only enemy that could assail them. Yes, I cried real tears!" Father's dream of the grandeur of a cottonwood forest, with all its luxurious variety of underbrush, shaded hammock, and picnic grove, was faded into the undisturbed silence of broken dreams.

In due time, the bonanza wheat crop of North Dakota was gathered and garnered, and its richness far surpassed the stub-pencil figuring of the farmers. The cloud from the steam threshing machine no longer floated across the blue canopy of the sky. The golden buff of the stubble outlined every gentle hillock on this, our lengthened lands. North Dakota was gilded with wheat, and now it was gilded with gold. The primitive beauty of our west was destined to lose some of her charm of wild sweetness and picturesque poorness, but she was rich in spirit and in romantic imagination, rich in bountiful goodness.

Most rich people in the world have one great fault, their "uninterestingness," but the people of the Sioux state forgot all past disappointments, and her people were interesting to themselves and to outsiders. They were buoyant with new life and elastic hopes for the future, and with all their richness they could still hold to the same old record: "nary a millionaire and nary a pauper!"

The bonanza year awakened the people of North Dakota to the wealth and beauty within their state and to the life-sustaining powers that slumbered in her soil and permeated her azonic air. Father said, in one of his soapbox political speeches in town: "The future of Stark County has a rainbow tied to its tail! It behooves every one of us who have vision and foresight to hang onto this rainbow and pull ourselves up by our boot straps until we reach that pot of gold! This can be a bubble world that the wind can break, or it can be a world within the world because nature has been here and left her mark, and she is here to stay!"

## Good Fortune for the Ranchers, Farmers, and Business

The spirit of prophecy hardly dares describe the visions of the bonanzan-ites for the grand and majestic prairies of the future. This was their land: their golden land where dollars came up out of the earth, and overactive must be the imagination that could outdo them in picturing a more outstanding future for their state.

There were changes—changes everywhere: changes in business and changes in individuals themselves. Those who were sure of themselves followed paths of promise to the fulfillment of their dreams. Far more became ranchers, and ranchers became farmers; those who had made their money on their land now wanted to be businesspeople in town; and small businesspeople in town had reaped a small fortune on their few outstanding acres, so they wanted more land and more room for expansion.

The few tender-footed and weak-kneed Jerseyites who had never gotten themselves acclimated, put their cash in their pockets, packed up their belongings, and went back to their beloved hills and valleys of the East. They said they wanted to see English daisies, sweet peas, mignonette, and clover bloom instead of cactus, buffalo grass, and Russian thistles. They wanted to get away from monotonous unpredictable winds that gave life and avidity to the ever-rolling and tumbling tumbleweed. It got into their hair and their whiskers, so they shook the gumbo from their feet. It was a good adjustment, and the real westerner came into his own, and the rancher and the farmer both had the same interests, and the western spirit predominated.

The wealth and prosperity of the Sioux state had been front-page news from coast to coast, and it brought an influx of new settlers who had long wanted some excuse to travel west. It also brought in many independent adventurers and soldiers of fortune and the professional hobos of the road. It brought the lazy vagabonds who entered into the whole-souled enjoyment of living on the fat of the land without working. It is a hard-earned case because it takes shrewdness of forethought with never an afterthought and boldness and nerve.

The little town of Taylor was in a real flourishing state of activity, and the very dust of the streets was stirred into a whirlpool of spontaneous commotion. Every day it looked as if a circus had come to town, and there were more human apes and monkeys on the streets than Barnum and Bailey ever held in captivity and enough jackasses running wild to start a wild herd of plains.

*Chapter Ten -*
# The A-BAR-B Ranch

This was father's description when he sold the Taylor Hotel and turned over the keys to the new proprietor, William J. Lacey, who was the richest wheat king of Stark County. Mr. Lacy had lived in the state for many years, and he knew from past records that the ups and downs of the climate cycle brought abundant production every seventh year. He believed it and preached it and acted upon it, putting every acre into cultivation that he could buy, rent, or just take because it was idle, weed-grown ground. Now he had reaped his reward.

He was the biggest booster for his state, but when a newspaper reporter tried to pin him down to the amount of wheat he had threshed and the amount he had received in dollars and cents, he calmly answered, "Why you seem to have your estimates all figured up, and I am taking your figures. You say we have seventy-eight million bushels of wheat and that netted a total of $175,000,000 for the North Dakota farmers! I have received my share out of that, out of this joy-giving wheat! I'll not trouble to be exact!"

"Don't you want to say something for the papers?" And then the reporter looked over the very old dilapidated buckboard and with plebeian insolence said, "Well, sir, don't you think you had better have your carriage newly painted?"

Mr. Lacy picked up his reins and drove off and called back; "Well, sir, you may call for this at any time and take it home and dye it! To hell with your newspaper! Get up, boney part!"

Father no longer held any township office; he was a total outsider, the owner and big boss of the A-Bar-B Ranch, five miles from Taylor. *Abraham Bloomfield Berry, Esquire,* they called him

[A. B. Berry]. He was an esquire in the true sense of the word—a landed proprietor. His rolling acres were all around him: a homestead claim, an irrigation of reservoir claim, and a tree claim with only a few scrubby withered and blackened cottonwood trees standing as witnesses for the government to justify the claim. But, he was a land baron and an esquire.

Berry was also the local land agent for railroad lands, and that gave him access to land that was not sold or in use. Altogether he had two thousand acres of verdant prairie land with indentations of ravines and gullies where water could be tapped that lay very close to the surface like deep reservoirs that are fed by subterraneous springs. It was not the usual hard water from the alkali springs but clear, pure drinkable water that needed no purification process of filtering.

This was an ideal location for the ranch. There were great rolling plains northeast from Taylor and then, a jumping off place, a deep ravine that ran jutted for miles across the country. Back in the glacial period there must have been grating and grinding of the ice masses to chisel out the irregular indentations in rock and earth.

Huddled close within the banks of this ravine were dense woods of trees and shrubbery ever watered by the hidden springs that would bubble forth here and there. This ridge of timber resembled the shores of a lake, indented with deep vistas like bays and inlets and, in some parts throwing out long points, like capes and headlands.

Below this ridge were thousands of acres of undulating prairie land with only the horizon line as a boundary, and on this plain was the A-BAR-B Ranch. No architect was needed to draw the plans for his ranch buildings. He hired three stalwart Norwegian carpenters, who, he said, excelled in brains and brawn, and they would follow his directions completely.

## The A-BAR-B Ranch

There was abundance of room, so nothing was to be crowded. Father would pace off the ground in one direction for the horse stables, in another direction for the cattle sheds, and the pigs and chickens could be closer neighbors. He left the entire west side free for his prospective sheep ranch; he knew the sheep would not be very popular with the other animals, which would not eat over the same pasture.

The construction and arrangement of the ranch house was entirely in Mother's hands, and with her mind based on practicality and beauty, she laid out a low rambling house that would be the butt of cyclonic winds. Mother laid out her plans with precision to bring all the comforts of a city home and yet be a step-saver. It was built in *L*s, and there was the east wing, west wing, and south wing.

Father would tease her: "Anne, I have to use a compass to find my way around this shack!" If he wanted us to bring something from the house, he would give directions thus: "It's in the northwest corner of the east wing, looking south!" or "It's in the southeast corner of the west wing, and if not, I'll be winged if I know which, where, and what wing."

The house became furnished in very exciting and much unexpected ways. The bedroom furniture and some of the living room furniture was brought from the hotel, and the curtains, draperies, and bric-a-brac were the precious things we had brought from Chester, New Jersey. Our home took on the warm Eastern atmosphere and quite away from the crude, wild-styled Western glare. Maple and I had moved our toys and dolls with us, but we were in the teens *[1895]* now and were trying to act like ladies.

A-BAR-B
Ranch
1895
Taylor
North Dakota

The stock of our ranch was also bought in very surprising and unexpected ways, and when Father left the ranch, we were all in a tether until he returned just to see what animal or animals or furniture he was bringing home with him.

"Thoroughbred." This was the word we heard every day when talking about stock and about people. "My stock must be thoroughbred, or, if not full-blooded, they must have a strain of the thoroughbred in them. This means high spirited and courageous, and these are the most desirable qualities in man and beast! I haven't got standing or lounging room for anything else."

Father had a way of mentally analyzing people, and he would speak of some neighbor: "I don't have any qualms about his actions or reactions because he is a thoroughbred!" And of another neighbor who had committed some misdemeanor in the community: "Poor devil, he is not responsible. His mongrel blood is following out its own destiny!"

## Hereford Cattle and Belgian Horses

Abram Berry scoured the country and into the adjoining states to buy stock for his ranch. He made many trips across the border into Canada, but he did not travel east as he said he wanted climate-sturdy stock. Our delighted surprise would come when he would return from a stock-buying trip as he would never bring back what he went after. At one time he went to Billings, Montana, to buy horses and returned with several pairs of twin heifers, fifty Plymouth Rock hens, two roosters, a Sleepy-Hollow rocking chair, and galvanized bread pans. Another time he went to South Heart to buy a flock of sheep, then he came home with some twenty mares of Belgian blood and a Scotch collie dog. He came by way of Dickinson, and there he purchased a new lounge for the living room. It was extra strong and reinforced with double springs and a dark-green corduroy covering. He told us: "Now don't scold me when I lay on this with my overalls and boots on. This is all I ask for of my own, and it will stand good hard wear and tear!"

The A-BAR-B was a horse and cattle ranch now but not on a very large scale. The cattle were mostly Hereford cows raising their own calves and a few Jersey cows that were milked and living an abundance of butter fat and rich cream. The cattle were Mother's investment. Her hobby was to buy twin calves, so Father was authorized and commanded, he said, to buy every pair of twin calves he could find. Once he came home with a pair of motherless twins so weak they could hardly stand. Their mother was killed by a timber wolf, and Father was riding cross country when he heard the cow bellowing. He got there just in the nick of time to save the helpless little animals as their mother died protecting them. He shot the wolf.

He solved the problem of how to take them home to the ranch. He made a sling with his coat and vest by tying the sleeves of his coat through the armholes of his vest, and with the rope he carried on his saddle, he securely held them on the back of his horse. This was one of our biggest surprises when he arrived home: the fact that he was riding one of his skittish horses, named Calico. This horse, a Clydesdale gelding, must have been cruelly treated when he was a colt broken to the saddle. He was afraid of every human being but Father. He so thoroughly distrusted humankind that there was a wicked gleam in his eyes when a stranger came near him. With Father he was as docile as a lamb or kitten, and his trust and confidence was never shaken. Calico had cantered home with his long strides; the coat and vest sling held firm and the twin calves did not feel enough life to make any resistance. The calves responded quickly to warm milk and a good rubdown.

Father shook out his coat and vests and wore them again. He said: "I really should write a testimonial to Montgomery Ward and Company. They advertised this suit in their catalog as 'a first-class businessman's suit, guaranteed to give satisfaction, for only $18.00.' I don't know what more I could ask of a suit besides wearing it!"

Father had set his heart on having a sheep ranch, and he had everything but the sheep. He was studying the different breeds of sheep to find the kind best suited for the rigorous climate of North Dakota. He was reading the *Breeder's Journal* and the *Dakota Farmer* and had all the reports from the North Dakota Agricultural College and had come to this conclusion: that he wanted the rugged Shropshire sheep as they had all the good points he was looking for, including the weight and height of the sheep, grade and quality of the fleece, the fact that they were rugged and sturdy with courageous endurance and mutton chops clear up to their necks. Now his quest was to find such sheep.

As all of Father's leaps into animal husbandry had been surprises, his break into the sheep industry was the greatest surprise of them all. That spring morning a passing rancher stopped at the A-BAR-B Ranch and left a handbill that claimed our attention at once. It was in large black lettering:

$100.00 R E W A R D!

IF YOU WILL RIDE INTO THE CIRCLE CORRAL AT TAYLOR ON SATURDAY AT 2 0'CLOCK PM. YOU WILL NOT GET THE ABOVE REWARD AND THAT MAN WHO THINKS HE CAN GET IT WILL FIND HIMSELF VERY MUCH MISTAKEN. BUT – YOU CAN GET THE BEST BARGAINS THAT HAVE EVER BEEN OFFERED AT AN
AUCTION SALE IN STARK COUNTY

HORSES – PONIES – CATTLE – SHEEP!
RANCHERS AND FARMERS DON'T MISS IT!
HEAR THE COWBOY BAND FROM BILLINGS, MONTANA

Father never missed a nearby auction sale, even if he did not want to buy the stock. He wanted to be sure that the animals were not abused or mistreated in any way. When he saw the handbill, he said that he was going in to look the sheep over, and he needed some herding ponies.

"You come along with me, Dottykins; you are the best substitute I have for a two-legged helper, and you have a simulated education for stock judging." I was elated and thought this a great compliment.

Saturday noon found us in Taylor, and it was a gala day for the whole county. Ranchers and farmers were coming in from the four points of the compass and coming in every sort of vehicle or on horseback. Cow punchers were riding up and down the streets, some giving exhibitions of their daring horsemanship, and cowgirls were attracting attention in their picturesque riding outfits.

Father and I had ridden in on horseback: Calico and St. Julian. We tied them in the barn of the Taylor Hotel. They were both too skittish to mingle in a crowd and too temperamental to sidestep with other horses. The herds to be auctioned off were held on the outskirts of town, and the air was filled with animal voices and echoes, and above all the din, the falsetto voices of the herders were heard calling to their helpers or yodeling or warbling their cowboy songs.

North Dakota was still a prohibition state, and there were no saloons in evidence, but there was plenty of hidden rotgut for those who knew the password. The Taylor Hotel and the section house across the tracks were the only eating places in town, and they were doing a rushing business as most of the people had left their homes early in the morning, and many of their herders had been in town all night.

There was a large sign on the porch of the Taylor Hotel, it read:

> Taylor Hotel, William J. Lacey, Proprietor. Travelers excursionists and others will find all the conveniences and comforts ample and agreeable. Charges moderate. Try us once and you will come again.

There was the menu card attached to this sign and in large lettering: "Dinner 50 cents. Home Brand of Cooking."

The section house displayed a large attractive sign on their porch:

> We invite everyone to partake of the social and solid comforts of this house. The proprietor may be found always attending to duties of the house, as landlord, and the table is the best that can be gotten. Prices are the most reasonable.

Dinner 40 cents, supper 35 cents, breakfast 25 cents. J.W.H. Cummings, Proprietor.

Both houses were well patronized with people waiting, but when the auction began, the crowd surged around the Circle Corral. Those who did not have time to get their dinner came out with sandwiches in their hands. The auctioneer, Big Walrus Wiggins, stood on a high platform near the gate of the corral, yelling to the top of his voice: "Right this way! Right this way! Come to the Vandu, gentlemen! Come to the Vandu!" Then he looked around and saw some women and children, so he made a very deep bow on each side of his rostrum: "Welcome, ladies. Welcome to the Vandu! Step right up and show these gentlemen that you know good stock when you see them! Show them who's boss of the ranch! Welcome, ladies!

If Walrus had any other name, no one knew it, but he did resemble a big bull walrus with his large bulk and his buck teeth with two fangs on either side, and they were always in evidence as his mouth was always open, either talking or laughing. Walrus had a resonant, cannon-like voice that had a far-carrying, reverberating sound that made him the most popular of auctioneers. He had a heart of gold and was also endowed with a King Solomon wisdom. He was the Mr. Anthony of those lengthened lands. He stopped Nancy from marrying a wild-drinking galoot from Mandan. He told Nancy that if she wanted to reform a man she must begin with his grandmother, and Nancy said, "He ain't got no grandmother."

Father found a seat for me on the west outside wall of the corral—a flat board that acted as a brace between two upright stanchions. Here I could look through the stallings at the animals in the corral and be safe from any danger, and I could look down on Walrus and on Father, who stood between the rostrum and the corral. I could see all the people I knew and wave to them. Biceps Joe rode up near and called out, "I see you're roosting high, Dotty! Now pick yourself a good pony!" I waved back.

I know good horseflesh when I see it, and I've ridden many a bucking bronco to break them from their cantankerous habits. It's not easy, but it sure is rewarding when you can gentle them with a firm squeeze of your knees and a strong love in your heart.

The excitement ran high when two skilled cowboys on well-trained ponies drove a bunch of mustangs into the corral. They were beautiful, quick-stepping, half-wind miniature horses from the plains. Some had been broken to saddle and bit; some had been badly treated and were broken in spirit and defiant of man; and some were untamed and unbroken and had fear and fire in their eyes, and they could not decide if man was their friend or their enemy.

## Auction Started for the Mustang Ponies

They would circle around the corral and whinny and stamp their feet. The voices of their herders were the only assurance they had that all was well. The two cowboys were lassoing the ponies and bringing them out to the gate in front of Walrus, and the bidding was on. It was not running very high as Indian ponies were very plentiful and horse-swapping and trading was the ranch loafers' pastime.

I talked to the ponies and put my hand through the stallings until several ventured up and trustingly nuzzled my fingers. A little dapple-gray gelding seemed the most intelligent and gentle of all, and after he had found me, he did not move around but kept near me. His soft nose would reach for my hand. When the cowboy came after him, he had only to lay the noose over his head. I was standing up now, waving wildly at Father and Walrus. They saw my frantic gesticulations, and Father seemed to be winking like mad. The bidding usually started at fifty cents, and some of the ponies had gone for two dollars, but the pony I wanted went on past, and Father kept on bidding by raising it a quarter or fifty cents.

There was a lull, and Walrus thundered out: "Going, going, gone, to Esquire Berry of the A-BAR-B Rancho for five silver cartwheels!"

"I crave a thousand pardons, Miss! I made a mistake; it is going, going, and *gone* again, to Miss Dorothy Berry of the A-BAR-B! Well, that's what it looks like to this old auctioneer!" I was overjoyed to have this pony, and the first name I thought of was Badger as he had the peculiar dark and light gray dappling *[marked with spots]* that resembled the cute little badgers. I led him out of the crowd and tied him to the stanchions *[an upright post]* of the corral.

Horses and cattle were auctioned off all afternoon, and Father did some bidding to keep the prices up to a reasonable amount, but he did not bid anything in. There was a lot of commotion around the gate as the cowboys urged the people atop to stand back and give more room, and then two herders and a dog brought in a flock of three hundred small Merino sheep, and Walrus started in with great gusto to call the crowd back.

"Come on, gentlemen! You can go home when you can't go anyplace else! Come to the Vandu! Come on, boys! What am I offered for these two-year-old ewes? What am I offered for this flock of mutton? Here is the beginning of a fortune! Three hundred ewes, all wool and mutton bearing! Here is wool on the hoof that will beat the tariff in Washington! Who wants to start a sheep ranch and run the cattlemen out of the country! What am I bid?"

There was laughing and bantering, yet the bidding was very low and very slow. Father stood near Walrus, and once in a while he would boost up the price. I looked over at him and saw him give several very pronounced winks, and then I waved at him to come and join me, and again he winked. Finally there was a lull, Walrus jumped up and down, almost falling off his rostrum, and his dog voice boomed out: "Sold! Sold to the self-appointed mayor of Taylor! Sold to that big man over there with the gold watch chain tethered to his vest. Sold to the big boss of the A-BAR-B! Three hundred sheep for three hundred Muzzukas!

"The Vandu is over! Thank you!" And he shook hands with himself and jumped off the rostrum. Father stood there speechless, and Walrus slapped him on the back with a hearty laugh: "I wish you luck, Berry, and I know they're thoroughbreds!"

"Thoroughbred scrubs! What have I ever done to you, Walrus, that you would hand this mangy flock of wool shedders down to me? I want sheep, but I don't want Merinos that you have to coddle and play nursemaid to all winter!" Father went into a sweat. His face was red, and he stood there mopping his head and neck down into his collar.

"Well, you gave me the wink, and what was I to understand by that? You gave me the wink when you wanted the pony, and you got it! You sure ain't flirtin' with me! I never failed a bidder yet! When anyone winks at me, I take him at his word! That's me, Walrus Wiggins!" And Walrus stood there with a puzzled look on his face. I had come over nearer, leading Badger and trying to understand what had happened.

Father sat down on the second step of the rostrum and looked at us. "What do you say, Walrus, that I winked at you?"

"That you did! With your right eye too! Jus' like this—" And Walrus gave a long, slow, downward pull of his upper-right eyelid.

"So that's what happened! I was afraid of that! That's no wink, Walrus; I've no business at auction sales. I've got a bad eye, Walrus. There are times when that eye can't behave! When I don't know it, that eye gets to twitching, and I wink and keep on winking. This eye used to get me in trouble with the girls. Many a time I had to take a girl home from the Christian Endeavor Society just because she said I looked across at her and gave her a wink. Now look! Here I've got just what I don't want to have and said I never would have in sheep! I preached about all the bad points of Merinos for this climate! How can I face my wife with such a scrubby bunch? How can I explain?"

Poor Walrus was feeling as sad as Father, and I was about ready to cry. The crowd had dispersed, and the three of us were left near the corral, looking dejectedly at the enclosed sheep that had suddenly become Father's property. "I'm sorry, Berry! I'm terribly mad inside at myself! Perhaps I count and depend too much on winks! Anyway, you got these sheep for a song, and you know, and I know, you can't sing a damn note! Take 'em home, partner, and we'll have another sale here in two weeks! If you don't want them then, bring them back, and I'll auction 'em off again. You can't lose, and you make some money!" There was nothing else to do. It was too late to take the sheep out to the ranch, so they were to stay in the corral all night. Father sent me to get the horses ready while he went to find a sheep herder.

"I know who I want. I want Ol' Skeets," whose real name was Thomas Skeeters, and he was one of the prairie-grown fixtures of Stark County. No one knew anything about Skeets's past, his parentage, or his environment. Only one thing he held onto positively: that he was born in "Nova Scotia." Just where that country lay geographically, he had no idea and would point toward it in any direction. He could not read or write but would fool any onlooker. He had no age look, and his worries and troubles touched him lightly, and he would give any number between twenty and thirty every time he was asked his age. No woman could beat him for keeping a youthful count.

I led Calico and St. Julian down to the corral, and they both looked with disdain at Badger. Father was standing there too dejected to move. "I wish these horses would give me a good kick for being such a blundering idiot as I was today! These Merinos originated in Spain, and I wish to heaven I could send them there!"

To Skeets, sheep were sheep, and he liked Father. Here was the fulfillment of his dream: to herd a flock of sheep and to have those sheep belong to A. B. Berry. His eyes were smiling, and his shaggy whiskers were shaking up and down. "That's a right fine bunch o' young ewes to lamb. I'll get 'em out early tomorrow mornin' an' get 'em through the gullies by the road, and bring 'em in to youse by night! Leave it to me! You can't learn me nothin' 'bout sheep herding."

"All right, Skeets! I'll depend on you to fill out the wrinkles!" And Father tried to smile.

We rode on home at a lively canter as our horses were impatient to get to their own stable and their bran mash. Father led Badger, and he trotted along with no fear. I had patted him and assured him that he was loved and in good hands, and his good "horse sense" told him the rest.

All the way home Father was trying to think how he would break the news of the Merino sheep to Mother. "She'll read the riot act to me for going against my good judgment! I've told her all the good points of sheep, and that I was going to buy some hardy thoroughbreds. This eye winking sounds too silly and sissified!"

We started in rather timidly to tell Mother and Maple about our day's adventure at the auction. They were both delighted with Badger, and when we said that we had three hundred sheep for three hundred dollars, they both began to praise Father with every adjective they could think of. They praised him for his keen insight, his sharpness in perpetrating a bargain, and for his vivid farsight because here was the proof. Now he could work out his thoroughbred breeding plans and raise sheep for both wool and mutton. Mother added, "Abie, you never buy like other people, just for the sake of buying. You always reason everything out, pro and con, and you always do the right thing at the right time; I never knew you to fail!"

Father did mention the wink and said, "It's a wonder Walrus did not throw everything in the auction at me the way my eye kept winking!"

And Maple piped up, "You just watch out, Daddy, or someday you will get something you don't want! Your eye seems to be more 'winkety' lately."

By the time the sheep arrived at sunset, we all seemed to be in a happier frame of mind. They looked good with their stomachs filled and their backs broad, and besides, we had no better sheep to compare them with. Father whispered to me, "I don't dare to look at a picture of a Shropshire, or I'll butcher this whole flock!"

A make-shift corral was made for the time being, and then the work on the ranch changed completely. The west side was laid out for a sheep ranch, and the three stalwart Norwegian carpenters came back to build the sheep sheds. Father paced them out just as he did the house and barns. Long low sheds extended around three sides and left a corral in the center, and this opened out into a very large feeding corral. The sheds had doors that lifted up, and this assured them complete protection in stormy weather.

It took Father about two years to build up a standard flock of three thousand Shropshire sheep. He kept the Merinos and bred them with his registered Shropshire rams, and the dark brown noses, ears, and feet predominated, and with their large square-built bodies, they made the little Merinos look like dwarf sheep. Whenever Father would see one of his original ewes, he would make some remark, such as: "Scat, you little animated drop of lanolin! You only got in here by a wink!"

Now the A-BAR-B Ranch was flourishing as a stock ranch and was advertised in many breeders' journals and was well patronized by the stockmen, and Father was often consulted on breeds of stock and their care. Every phase of our ranch life was vital with a human interest for every living thing on it. The winter of 1895, Berry wintered 1,100 head of sheep with only a loss of three. He told the newspapers when he was interviewed, "That there is a brighter prospect for the sheep industry, and the man who holds onto his flock is the man who will win."

# Abram Berry-A North Dakota Legend

**CHOICE BREEDING STOCK ALWAYS ON HAND. FOUNDATION STOCK a Specialty**

## A. B. BERRY

*Breeder and Importer of Registered* **SHROPSHIRE SHEEP**

CAN FILL ANY ORDER ON SHORT NOTICE. RANCH FIVE MILES FROM TAYLOR
VISITORS MET AT TRAIN
BY APPOINTMENT ∴ Also *Breeder and dealer in Draft Horses*

Taylor, N. Dak., _____ 190__

LETTERHEAD of the A. B. Berry Sheep Ranch

Copied from "WHO'S WHO" of American Writers

Dorothy de St.Clement  (Countess Dorotes de Sauteiron de St.Clement)
30 Daily Street, Nutley,10, New Jersey

    Born in Short Hills,New Jersey (on a farm) When 5 years the family,father A.B.Berry, mother, Annie Berry; and Maple and Dorothy moved to Taylor, North Dakota. Had the Taylor Hotel. Later had a sheep ranch 5 miles northeast of Taylor. Attended the North Dakota Agricultural College at Fargo and taught school in a prairie school house in Stark County, North Dakota.

    Literary career started from childhood. Contributed stories and poems for local papers and for the Children's Page of Magazines. While at College wrote articles for Farm papers on Animal Husbandry and Stock Raising etc.

    Married an Italian Nobleman from Rome Italy; Count Giulio de Sauteiron de St.Clement who became a Naturalized Citizen. He was connected with the Italian Steamship Lines in New York and Chicago.

    Lived in Rome, Italy from 1921 to 1938, coming back every 2 years for a short stay and to keep our citizenship.

    Started writing for Italian newspapers of the States.La Tribuna d'Italia and The Italian Tribune and syndicated a Column "Travel Talks" while traveling the Continent.

    Contributed Short Stories to Progress Magazine, a Unity Publication of Kansas City, Missouri.

    Sold Short Stories to "Porto Rico Illustrado" San Juan, Porto Rico. stories were translated in Spanish.

    Have been free-lancing short-stories, articles, and poetry for 20 years and in 1951 first book WHITE GUMBO was published by Vanfage Press,
120 West 31st, Street,
New York City.

*Chapter Eleven -*
# Cowgirls Go to New Jersey

Father's philosophy was so sound and so satisfying, and we proved it many times in those wonderful changing days. His churchless religion meant just as much to us. He would say: "My church is outdoors, under the great canopy of the sky, and God is my preacher."

Father and Mother made a great sacrifice to send us two girls away from them. Youth cannot understand but only accept. Life moved on very quickly, it seems, from the Taylor Hotel to the A-BAR-B Ranch and into our grown-up days. Maple was happy now in New Jersey; she finished her course in the business college. She was in love from her school days and through college with *William James Frost,* a very handsome and educated young man. Will was studying law and working in a law office. His father had acres of timber land and also owned a saw mill. Maple and Will were married and moved to Dayton, Ohio, where Will had an executive job, and they soon had a nice little home there.

I had finished her college course in Fargo, North Dakota, and was happy to be back on the A-BAR-B Ranch again with all the animals. My studies were in stock raising, stock breeding, and judging at the North Dakota Agricultural College. I was an expert in animal husbandry, but there didn't seem to be any ladylike jobs offered to me.

Where could I find a ladylike job on the prairies? Father racked his brains about this and finally came up with this solution: "School teaching seems to be about the only answer for you, my Dotty dear. But you should have graduated from a normal school, and then you would be completely prepared! Why, Dotty, you'll have to take the teacher's examination for this!

I loved to write and was constantly sending poetry, short stories, and articles to various markets. Occasionally I would receive a check, and then we would have a whopping celebration. Father would remark, "You'd better take the school exam, Dotty!" In early June, I was offered the Jesperson School near Taylor—the largest and best paying school around. It was considered a difficult school, with thirty pupils—all boys of an unruly age—and they preferred a strong man for the teacher position. Anyway, I agreed to take the teacher's examination in August and teach there at the school in September.

Father and Mother had been mumbling to each other over breakfast, lunch, and dinner about what I was going to be doing after the summer. I could tell they were ready for another family powwow. Sure enough, those two dears pushed me into the living room and onto the couch, then made themselves comfy in their favorite chairs nearby.

"Now this is it, Dotty! Your Mother and I have been ruminating! We have kept this a big surprise! My trip to Taylor yesterday was not all butter and eggs and selling a ram! I did a little on-the-side business. I have bought you a return ticket to Newark, New Jersey. You'll have to buy another ticket on that "Rock-a-Bye-Baby Railroad," and that takes you rockety-rolling to the hidden-away town of Chester, New Jersey. You can't even find it on a map! You are going to a jumping-off place! You can have six weeks there and get back for the teacher's examination in Dickinson in August."

You will be with Maple and Will as they leave in August for their new home in Dayton, Ohio. This is the nicest way for you to thank your grandparents for their help in buying you the things you've needed to prepare for your job." I was in ecstasies of joy and overflowing happiness. I hugged both so hard that they screamed, and the dogs came to the door to protect whoever needed protecting!

I started packing right away; I would take my pigskin bag and my tourist trunk. I'd have to pack a few Indian curios to take as gifts. Father can put in a bag of North Dakota potatoes in my trunk for a family Sunday dinner in New Jersey.

This was another time to bid the animals good-bye; but there was not much ceremony as they were getting so used to it that they were cold and indifferent. Again, there was a big scene in Taylor at the station. Father always drove in with his horses prancing, but when they saw my trunk on the platform of the station, all the people flocked over to see me! "Where and why are you going away again? Come back soon! You've got a school for this fall! Don't get yourself married!" The train pulled in, and I was helped into the parlor car. I waved and threw kisses, and I knew that Father would explain to them where I was heading again.

My six weeks in New Jersey were as wild and wooly as two western girls could make it. We were taken from place to place to visit relatives and friends. Everyone seemed surprised to see us so up to date in clothes and manners and in every way. In many ways we had a broader outlook than our eastern cousins. We found out that some of them were almost afraid to have us come back. They expected some wildness as we grew up around cowboys and Indians.

We shared stories about the Middle West being populated with the nicest class of people from many European countries: home-loving, energetic, and prosperous settlers. These settlers were raising their children with all the advantages of eastern families—like our family, who had a broader opportunity to own land of their own. Father owned two thousand acres; and where could you find two thousand acres to homestead in New Jersey? Maple and I shared a lot of stories about the West, and they liked hearing about the Sioux Indians most of all.

## Dorothy Dresses Formal for Parties

We were invited to several home parties. There was one outstanding party that changed the whole tenor of my life. My Uncle

Ike and Aunt Jane lived in the most aristocratic section of Newark, New Jersey. I thought it was a palace: a three-story red brick building on a beautiful street with trees and a park nearby. There were six children in the family, all different ages. Several were grown-up young ladies, and their daughter Olive was a college student my age.

Dorothy Berry de St. Clement – 1906 in Nutley, New Jersey

I was preparing to return to North Dakota when Cousin Olive informed me that she was giving a farewell party for me; so I could meet some of her friends. She would invite friends from New York

City and also two Italian noblemen from Italy: one named Count Giulio de Sauteiron de St. Clement from Rome and the other a Baron Andrea de Bonifacio from Milan, Italy. She said that they were both wonderful men and that the count spoke very good English, his mother being English and his father, French. I was told that they had a castle in the northern part of Italy and that the count lived in New York City at present and speaks nine languages fluently. Olive confessed that she really didn't know them, but that they were friends of her sister, Grace. She said that she wrote about "me" in the invitation because she wanted them to meet me. Olive said, "Oh, Dotty, wear your beautiful blue ruffled dress with the pearl trimming, your gold shoes, and long white gloves. And fix your golden hair hanging in curls."

I was so nervous since it was a type of party I had never attended before. I felt I would be dressed right, but all the things I was supposed to do worried me. Olive had me practice walking down the long stairway, slowly pointing my toes out when halfway down; I would turn my head and look into the reception room and smile. Then I would sort of hurry, and Olive would reach out her hands to meet me and introduce me. She would say, "My dear friends, this is my cousin Dorothy Berry from North Dakota!"

I loved it, but I was very nervous as Olive explained: "This will be the biggest surprise! They are expecting to see you look like a cowgirl and to act sort of wild, like an Indian or a western girl! I'll show them—my western cousin is a lady!"

While I was wrought up trying to act the part to please Olive, I knew what Father and Mother would say: "Just act natural and be yourself. Don't try to act like something you are not."

So I consoled myself, *I am not trying to please those two foreign gentlemen.*

Maple would not even come near this party, and I'm glad she didn't. The whole thing was a bit embarrassing to me, but Olive was doing this for me, so I would do my best and go through it to please her. It would be fun to tell this to Father and Mother when I got back home on the A-BAR-B Ranch.

Interestingly, Olive was coaching me how to walk gracefully with a little swing, how to sit in a chair so my skirts would spread gracefully, and to keep my feet and ankles at a nice angle. I had to curtsy *[a woman's bow of greeting]* to each guest as introduced and to shake hands at a high altitude just to touch with the tips of my fingers. We did our elite-company manners quietly by ourselves first so that Aunt Jane and the family did not see us practice.

That evening Olive told me I was a fast learner in social etiquette. It was all quite suspenseful because Olive kept me on the third floor and away from the lower parts of the house. She said "the refreshments were perfectly divine." A light supper was brought up to me in my room; then I started to dress for dinner. Makeup had not become a part of my dressing up. I only knew to use a dusting of pale pink powder over my face to assure that I had no shine. My golden hair was brushed out in loose curls. My blue ruffled dress came down to my shoe tops, and my jewelry consisted of a chain and locket, a bracelet, and a gold ring with my birthstone. My white gloves reached to my elbow; and I left those for the last thing to put on. Now I was ready to descend the stairway to the second floor.

I could hear laughter and happy voices as the company started to arrive. I had expected more quiet decorum than this. Then I thought, *Parties are parties and Olive seems to know all about them.* This gave me a more confident feeling, and I became less nervous.

Cousin Clyde, who was ten years old, came up to get me, and there was something very dubious about his expression when he saw me. He walked with me to the second floor. I looked down and saw Olive standing in the hallway. From there I put on my act. I descended to the first floor with my toes pointed and my smile all set. Olive was looking up at me with looks of approval. As I reached the center of the stairway, I turned my head and was all ready for flashing and beaming a smile, but that smile froze on my face!

The great hall doors were open now, and the living room was filled, packed tight, not with the elite and four hundred of New York City ladies and gentlemen, but with cowboys and cowgirls, all dressed in the paraphernalia of Western range-style clothes! They were wearing blue jeans, short skirts, and shirtwaists, and all had red and yellow bandanas around their necks. Sombreros and twirling long ropes, quirts, and a few toy guns were popping along with a few noisemakers. All of them greeted me with war whoops and loud cheers. Then I saw there were a few Indians mixed in. It was a real Western greeting in every way.

It was a terrific shock, but it was a happy shock—a great relief to know that I did not have to go on putting on the "dog" and painfully going through all the etiquette I had been practicing all these days. It took me a few minutes to get composed since it was a shock!

I gave a war whoop as I ran down the stairs, pulling off my long gloves. I lost my gold slippers on the stairs, but I was no longer conscious of myself. They were all around me, hollering "Surprise!" They were all of Olive's friends, and I couldn't believe that I knew most of them. Now I was sorry that Maple was not here. With all the cheering and laughing I seemed to sense that something was really missing. It was my sister, Maple. Oh how I missed her that night.

Then I thought that something else had been forgotten! It was! "Oh, Olive, where are your two noblemen?"

Olive came to her senses and felt a little confused and embarrassed and grabbed me. She took me aside and said, "Oh, Dotty, they are mad! I can't talk to them! They don't understand this joke! Come with me!" We walked back into the living room. Standing there with their backs against the wall stood two young men dressed in business suits. They pulled themselves up very stiffly, and the expression on their faces was livid.

It was the most embarrassing moment I ever experienced. I looked at them. I was trying to smile, but I knew my expression was one of bewilderment. Olive had already tried to explain; now she was trying to apologize. Pulling me over very close to her, she said, "Your highness, I want you to meet Miss Dorothy Berry from North Dakota. This is a surprise party for her, and she is very surprised. This is a joke. All of the guests thought it would be a Wild West party, but we told Dorothy this was a very reserved, fashionable party with the elite of New York society here and two gentlemen of nobility from Italy.

"You see how surprised my poor little cousin is? My poor cousin was so shocked she almost fell down the stairs. Did you see her? Excuse me; I cannot say your names. Will you please introduce yourselves? Sister Grace does not know I invited you gentlemen. I know she is going to be very angry with me; but I wanted this big surprise for my western cousin!"

The baron stood stupefied. He could not understand the whole situation. The count gradually got control of himself; he was so bent with anger that he could not speak coherently. He stuttered, and then he got angrier. He took my hand and kissed it and then held it as he looked at me. "I cannot apologize enough for your rude cousin. This is a deplorable situation. I am so sorry for you. It was a terrible ordeal to put you through. I am very angry. This arouses all my French, Italian, and English blood. I am fighting mad. Miss Olive, I don't think you understand what an abominable joke you played on such a nice cousin. I cannot find words in your language to tell you what you have done. You have insulted your cousin. I will talk to Grace about you. My friend and I do not want any part of this asinine joke."

He was still holding my hand, and he turned to me and talked very close to my ear. "I apologize to you. You handled this quite well and saved her party. I admire you very much. I will see you again. I will find you, piccina mia!" As he bent low to talk in my ear, he kissed me on my hair and hurriedly left the room with the baron following close. He even slammed the outside door as he let the baron out.

We all stood as if in shock. I wished I could have gone out that door with him. I was in no mood for a party after that. When Olive told me that she was giving a "surprise party to outdo all surprise parties," she really did.

The party went on then, and not one person mentioned the titled and very aristocratic gentlemen. Then it became thoroughly western. I went upstairs and changed into western clothes: short skirt, shirtwaist, and a red bandana handkerchief tied in a knot around my neck. I even found Clyde's cowboy hat; so there I was, looking like I was at the A-BAR-B Ranch (my home).

We rolled up the hall rug, and we danced there. Olive's oldest sister Nellie played for us, all the popular dances and jigs and a waltz. The party was not loud or boisterous; the nobility incident had put a damper on foolish gaiety, and there was quiet and good behavior. Our fabulous refreshments were served western style: buns with ham and cheese, doughnuts, and lemonade and orange juice. The party even broke up early as there was no longer any enthusiasm to hold it together. Olive was conscious stricken; I was walking on a cloud.

Olive and I went up to the third floor to sleep. We were strained toward each other, and finally I said: "Olive, the count was so sorry for me, he kissed my hand. (I did not mention the kiss on my hair)."

Olive gave a little shrug and laughed, "You poor little western thing, why, he kisses every girl's hand. Those foreigners mush over every girl. It's all the same to them. The count was putting on a big act because he was so enraged at me. Ha-ha! I don't care if I ever see him again. I don't know how I am going to explain everything to Grace. She will punish me because Grace never sees things as I do!"

I went to bed with a heavy heart. It was a very rude joke when I thought it over. I know Father and Mother would think the same. I did not wash my "kissed hand" that night, and I went to sleep in a dream land of knights and ladies holding their hands high and dancing the minuet, and then little lambs were jumping a fence, and I was asleep.

The next morning when I was trying to excuse it all, a telephone call came for Olive. As soon as I heard her hysterical giggles, I knew who was at the other end of the phone line, and I kissed my hand.

## Count Giulio Invites Dorothy to New York City

Olive was holding the telephone receiver, and she turned to me and said, "Dotty, Count Giulio and the baron are inviting us to come to New York City tomorrow morning and spend the whole day with them and even have dinner at night. They will see us to our door, will you come?"

Olive was giggling and laughing and gushing and delivered my simple little answer, "Yes" but I was jumping up and down saying "goody, goody, I'm so glad!"

Then Olive said, "He was very cool."

She tried to imitate the count in staccato words: "I am not apologizing to you. Your party was abominable, but I want you to bring your lovely cousin to New York. We will try to atone for the atrocious joke you imposed upon her and her sweet nature."

The next morning, Olive and I went to New York City on the ferry boat, and the two noblemen were at the dock to meet us. When we stepped off the ferry onto the dock, Giulio took my arm. Olive hitched right on to the arm of Baron Andres. They both were very poised, stiff, and polite. They had hired a taxi cab for the day, and we were taken to every place of interest. The inside tours of the Statue of Liberty thrilled me the most. I took notes on everything we saw and did because I planned to give these events in detail to my school children in the Jesperson School—and to all my friends.

Count Giulio took us to the Italian steamship office where he was employed. They took us around the harbor in a small boat. Giulio was the interpreter for this Italian line, and he entertained us by telling us words and phrases in different languages and even singing some songs for us. Baron Andrea sang songs in Italian and French. We were so entranced with their voices; we just never expected to be entertained like that.

We were delighted with the aquarium. I took down all the information I could find and tried to remember all the things Giulio explained to us.

We had lunch in an Italian restaurant in the business section. It was a very cheerful atmosphere with laughter and music and bantering in different languages. To me, it was a place in another world. In the afternoon we spent time visiting the great stores on Fifth Avenue. We also were taken through Chinatown, and that was quite unique. To share these points of interest from the harbor to the top of the skyscrapers with the children in North Dakota, I would have to use some good descriptive explanations, especially to the ranchers who have never been to the East Coast or to any big cities. For dinner they took us to another Italian restaurant. It was very home-like; it was "Mamma Leone's." Everyone seemed to know her and called her "Mamma." The count introduced us. She was pleased that I had come such a long way from home. She smiled and pinched my cheek.

All through the day, Giulio tried to impress me very sincerely that he was very much interested in me. He said that he was very much in love with me. He was planning to visit our ranch in August and talk with my parents. He said that it had to be this way as he could not talk of love to me until he had the permission of my parents. He said that I was only a child in years—and a baby in experience. I was very surprised and yet in my heart I knew the moment I saw him at the party that he was someone very special. I laughed to myself to think of my Father and Mother meeting him. He did not know how I had been brought up. If I were to marry him, it would be my decision: Father would take me aside and ask me, "Dotty, do you want to marry this man?" and I would say, "Yes, Father, I found him at a crazy party in Newark, New Jersey." And Father would say, "Well, okay, if you know what is in your heart, then I approve."

We did not tell Olive or the baron the secret we held. In fact, I did not tell Maple. I would wait to see how this developed, with all respect to Father and Mother as well as my Giulio.

The next day I was back in Chester with Maple and my grandparents. I told them details about my visit and trip to New York City but kept the little secret. We spent a busy week, and by the end of the week I was back in Newark to take the Northern Pacific Railway train to St. Paul, Minnesota, and on to Taylor, North Dakota.

*Chapter Twelve -*
# Going Home to Teach School

A homecoming in Taylor was just like a circus coming to town. When the incoming train rolled into Taylor, everyone in town was at the station or standing all along the street or on the porches of every store. No one could sneak into town when taking the Northern Pacific.

When my train rolled in at two o'clock in the morning, I almost jumped right into Father's arms as he stood next to the conductor, who was helping me with my baggage—my dear old pigskin bag. I felt something rubbing against me, and I looked down. It was Emil, my dog, who had left the buggy and had followed Father. Emil was well mannered so we never had to scold him.

Everyone was calling to me: "Hi, Dotty!" "Hello, Miss Berry. Glad to see you back! We got your school all clean and waiting. We were afraid you'd get married back there." One old fellow called out, "You're getting prettier all the time, Dotty Berry! Wish I was a young colt; I'd keep you out here." This brought on more bantering, "Look who's talking." Everyone was happy and laughing. When I kissed the dog, there was more bantering. "Don't waste your kisses on your dogs and horses anymore, Dotty. You're all grown up."

"I'm old enough to give you good and sensible advice." This comment came from a long-time friend, an old sheep herder of ours.

I patted him on the back. "Thanks for the sensible advice."

Everyone was waving as I climbed up on Father's red-wheeled buggy with Emil as he crowded in between us, and I waved goodbye. It was wonderful to be home again, but I felt that I was a changed person. I felt so thoroughly grown up now.

We were a very open family, so I had to tell my experiences of my time in New Jersey in every detail. They usually praised my diplomatic handling of most situations but were shocked and amused with my acted-out description of Olive's farewell party. "It would be Olive's way of celebrating."

Father laughed long and loud. "Just think of all the free and footloose young men in New York, and she found those two Italian noblemen, whom she knew through Grace, and invited them to a Western hoedown!"

"Oh, Father, it was a scream and so embarrassing for those two polite gentlemen, and they were so angry. And then the count kissed my hand, right here."

Then Father said, "That was his noble breeding, Dotty girl. You looked like a little bunch of timothy hay blown in there with that whole mess of buffalo grass! To put it stronger, you looked like one of Juliette's shoats *[a young weaned pig]* standing there in that herd of demented razorback hogs."

I could not get settled into any of the serious activities of the ranch. I could not get control of my feelings inside. I was just dancing around doing things that did not need to be done. Outside, I walked from building to building, lingered in the stable, and talked foolishly to the horses until they gave me looks of disdain. No human could have said more things without words than I.

## The Count Comes to Dickinson, North Dakota

Now I was making all the plans for my teacher's examination in Dickinson and for my nobleman friend to visit there at the same time.

Mother was urging me on with advice. Mother would say, "Don't forget to take your prettiest dresses since you will be there for five days." And, "Take May with you wherever you go; don't leave May out since you are visiting her. Let May's father, Sheriff Hayes, make all the arrangements for your nobleman's visit for him to stay at the St. Charles Hotel. The sheriff can see that they do special things for his comfort."

"Oh, Mother dear, I think he's going to be interested and amused with everything here, especially if he makes the comparison of Taylor with Australia. I feel sure we have more advancement here. The St. Charles Hotel is so homey, and the proprietor is so kind. She makes the hotel feel like a home."

Annie replied, "You know what your father says: 'We make our own life. We bring either good or bad upon us according to how we think and how we live. We must thank God continually for all the good that comes to us.'"

"Mother, now I know that I must keep a level head to get through that examination. The train will be in at three o'clock, and I can't get to the hotel until five o'clock. Giulio will only have to stay at the hotel one night. Then we will be in Taylor on the ten o'clock train the next morning. Would you see that Father comes in with the red buggy shining and his horses prancing so that will be the way we go out to the A-BAR-B?"

The day arrived for me to spend my week in Dickinson. I was walking on air and trying to make excuses for my nervousness. I thought to myself, *I have two reasons for going away.* Then I realized that I was really absent-minded. I put the tea kettle on the stove without water. Then I burned the cake. I scorched the omelet. Then after I was dressed, I realized that my shoes didn't match. I needed to get a hold of myself and remember not to put anything on my face so that I would look natural. Who was I fooling? I was a nervous wreck.

Well, I arrived in Dickinson on the three o'clock afternoon train, and May Hayes was at the station to meet me. She was just as thrilled as I was since she knew about my meeting with Giulio in New Jersey; I had written her everything. We jumped up and down, talking and laughing with exhilaration. She said her father had arranged our visit in big style to entertain nobility. The sheriff made all the arrangements. He would entertain the Italian count and show him the town of Dickinson. May said that we could be there by five o'clock and have dinner in the dining room.

May said, "They will have a little table in the corner for both you and the count." And she wouldn't tell me what the townsfolk had planned. But she did say it will be a real Western event because all of Dickinson knows an Italian nobleman is visiting.

May showed me that she had his full name written down correctly: *Count Giulio de Sauteiron de St. Clement from Rome Italy and New York City*, so the town and the newspapers would have it right. And it would also state that he was the guest of Miss Dorothy Berry and the Sheriff Hayes family. They also knew that he was going to visit the A-BAR-B Ranch for a week, which was right outside of the town of Taylor.

Western hospitality was at its height the next day when the nobleman arrived on the westbound train. Sherriff Hayes had a good turnout of men, women, and children at the station to give him a rousing western welcome.

The count bowed and smiled and thanked the sheriff and everyone for their coming to welcome him to their town. He was escorted to the St. Charles Hotel. They explained to "his highness" with apologies that North Dakota was and had been a prohibition state for many years, but they had a very nice "Red Plush" private place where they could serve him all the French and Italian wines. Count Giulio was very much amused and thanked them for their sincere interest in his welfare. He was very impressed.

All this time May and I were bent over our desks, taking our tests in the county courthouse. The courthouse stood on the highest point in Dickinson, so we could see out the window and watch the smoke from the engine as it was approaching the town of Dickinson. When it passed over Young Man's Butte, it looked like a volcano erupting. Then the trail of smoke came nearer and nearer, and we could tell when the "chug-chug" stopped at the station. It was a wonder that we could keep our minds on our exams.

We would read a question and then search around in our minds for the answer. It was surprising how our poorly divided thoughts could even concentrate. We both passed the examination with honors and received our teaching certificates. Father said, "I prayed for you because you were obviously very nervous when you left the ranch. So God put a guardian angel over you." May said that the angel helped her too.

May and I went to her house so we could change our dresses and get ready for the evening. We did not put on any makeup since Sheriff Hayes was even more outspoken than Father about young girls looking natural. They both agreed that it was much more ladylike. They didn't believe in looking "painted up."

We both hurried over to the St. Charles Hotel. Then May suggested that I go up to the parlor floor alone. So I did so with a nervous and insecure feeling. I knocked on the door of the bridal suite, and to my relief there was no answer. I slowly pushed the door open to peek inside; sure enough there was no one there. I returned to the first floor to look for May. May decided that I should return to the lobby and wait for the count to appear, and she would come back later for the evening. May was dancing around, saying, "I know there is going to be something wonderful for this evening."

I waited in the parlor of the hotel as if on pins and needles, pinching myself and questioning myself: "How did I ever get myself mixed up with Italian aristocracy? What is going to come of this?" Then before I could look up, two strong arms picked me up out of my chair, pressed me to him tightly, kissed me on top of my head, stood me on my feet, and looked smilingly into my face.

I stuttered, trying to make some nice comment, and we both laughed. We tried to talk happily and naturally in the same vein as we had been corresponding for several months.

He took my arm and escorted me down stairs to the dining room. The count had met everyone, and the staff were all bowing to him and to me. I had never felt so very insecure—but important—before. Oh how I wished Father and Mother were here. I missed them and needed them more than ever in my life now.

Every table in the dining room was filled. So I knew now the news had spread around that an Italian nobleman was at the St. Charles Hotel. It was a surprise to both of us as we had hoped to be by ourselves. Our gracious hostess made a very nice announcement: "A nobleman is here this evening, and we welcome him with our Western hospitality." Everyone cheered and stood up, and some called us in a friendly way, smiling and watching our every move.

For a fraction of a second I saw a very fixed and almost indignant look in Count Giulio's eyes (the look I had seen at Olive's Party). It changed just as immediately to a gracious smile and even a twinkle in his eyes. He then did a slight bow of recognition and made a nice speech: He was from Italy; he was very grateful for a position he held in New York City and very pleased to be visiting very dear friends in North Dakota.

We were ushered to our secluded table in a corner of the dining room. He was amused because our coffee cups held red wine, and no one knew it. We tried to talk happily, and I tried to break the news to him that he must be patient and submit to whatever entertainment the town had planned for us tonight. These western people were so big-hearted and wanted to do all they could for him. I said, "You must be happy and show them your appreciation. Express all the joy you can, my dear Giulio," I pleaded.

He gave in, "I will not disappoint you, *piccina mia*. I did not come here for parties or even to see anyone else—just you and your folks."

He continued: "I have just come here to see your dear parents. Will they trust me with one of their most precious possessions?

I have sent you my mother's letters so that you know what she thinks, and she loves you now. We have learned a lot about each other through our letters, and your parents have read my letters, and you have read my mother's letters, so we both understand."

We had just finished our dinner when May and all her friends came to see us. They were all beaming as they were introduced. I was happy to see that Giulio put on such a gracious response. He was more than gracious. He pulled May close to us, and he praised her father, the sheriff, for his escort to all places of interest in Dickinson.

Everyone was talking and laughing as we all meandered out into the hall. The sheriff stood there to welcome us. He mounted a soapbox and with his arms extended, and his voice boomed out: "Listen, ladies and gentlemen of Dickinson. We have a very distinguished visitor, Count Giulio. I will just call him this, if I may have his permission, because I cannot pronounce his complete name. But you can read it on our register. I wish we had a grand opera to entertain him. Let us be truly Western. We have a very nice merry-go-round in town. Our young and old citizens have been enjoying it. We have rented it for two hours from eight to ten o'clock, and all adults are invited to enjoy it. We are sorry, but just tonight no children are allowed to be on the merry-go-round. This is a time to honor our guest, Count Giulio, and our own cowgirl, Dorothy from the A-BAR-B Ranch. Follow me! We are going there now!"

## Let's Go Ride the Merry-Go-Round

I was afraid to look at Giulio's face. He was smiling, holding up his hand, and he spoke in his beautiful cultured voice with great sincerity. "My dear people of Dickinson, I am overwhelmed with this surprise, mingled with appreciation and joy. I have just come to your town, and I feel I am one of you. This western spirit is so kind and enveloping. I must tell you the truth: I hope to make this sweet cowgirl my wife! That is why I am going to the A-BAR-B

Ranch. Thank you from the bottom of my heart for this demonstration of friendship."

There was a lull—a moment of silence; and before it could all sink in, the sheriff boomed out, "Come on, hombres! Follow me!" Both May and I took Count Giulio by his arms, and we all marched out of the hotel, went down the street, and turned the corner, and then we could hear the calliope!

There were many calls of congratulations for Giulio, but they could not get through to him. They flocked around us and all hoping that the count would come west to live. Our answer was to these questions: "We hope we will be able to." I was very proud of my nobleman, to see him adapt himself to this terrific expression of friendship. It was not just a casual expression; I felt that it was genuine. I knew that he felt the sincerity of this Western spirit, and he was trying his best to show his own appreciation in return. Now I knew I loved him. I had a true glimpse of his innermost soul before it was seen outward.

The merry-go-round was the first-model type: double seats of bright red plush with two rows of spirited-looking horses with fancy saddles and bridles. These horses' faces looked just like our dear horses at home. All of the outside riders would reach for the ring, which, if reached and taken, would give them a free ride. I was pleased to see how the count adjusted himself to the spirit of this entertainment. We sat on the plush seats of the merry-go-round, and he put his arm around me and would hum or sing with the music, and everyone was pleased. We also tried the ponies for one ride. After that I insisted that he ask some of the girls to ride with him. He did so with a humble smile. There would be a ladies' choice, and the girls would come after him. May had her chance, and even the sheriff's wife made them all laugh when they rode the horses, and the count caught a free ring; even with all the free rides. It was so much fun.

Ten o'clock came before we realized it, and there was an outside crowd of people waiting to take over the merry-go-round. I was hoping to go back to the hotel with Giulio, but I had no choice; all the plans were made for us. Our little group was escorted to May's home by the sheriff and his wife. There was just time for a "good–night" and "pleasant dreams" song, and then they all left us. This group of young people had planned to take the count back to the hotel and plague him with many questions. He told them about his French father and his English mother and their beautiful castle in northern Italy, in the foothills of the Alps. He told them it was run like a little village. All the people who lived there had their own little cottages and worked on the land. He said that they also had a little chapel and a small theater. It was a village he called Berthamond.

They wanted to know: If he planned to marry me, would we live there? The count said that he hoped that someday we would live there, but just now he was connected with the Italian steamship lines, and he had to live in Rome and also in New York City. That was where he would take "his little western girl." He also said that they would always have a "standing invitation to visit us wherever we lived." They all agreed to keep in touch with us. The count promised that he would come back to North Dakota and really wished that he could live out here too. The count also told them of his many amusing experiences in Australia, with his aunt and uncle on a sheep ranch. He had them all laughing at his tenderfoot experiences. He said that the cowboys could go him one story better.

Night settled down over the prairie lands of North Dakota. May and I had talked on into the night. Count Giulio had settled down in his clean hotel bed. The cool night breezes swept through the window; to the westerner it was always so: no matter how hot the days were, the nights were balmy and cool.

The next morning Sheriff Hayes escorted Count Giulio to the railway station, which was just across the street from the hotel. May and I arrived in good time and gathered friends along the way. Many who joined us were friends from the evening before. The station platform was filled, and the line extended along Villard Street. I was happy to find Giulio in the same jovial mood. He seemed to have embraced the spirit of the West and was using cowboy and western expressions.

When the train rolled in, there was wild cheering. Then as we boarded, everyone waved and yelled out "farewell."

Then Giulio responded, "So long, hombres, I'll see you at the roundup!"

This brought wild cheers and laughter as they yelled again, "Come again; please come back again."

## Taylor Is Only Two Stations Away

We watched our Dickinson friends as the train went around the bend. Taylor was only two stations away, and I knew that Father and Mother would be there waiting for us in his red-wheeled wagon. We arrived at the station in Taylor, and the platform and streets were filled with friends and lots of townsfolk, but I couldn't see Father. Jim Goldsberry pushed through the crowd, took my hand, and reached up to shake hands with Giulio.

"I welcome you, your highness. I apologize for Abie Berry; he was not able to come to greet you." Turning to me, he said, "Dorothy, your father could not leave the ranch. There are some things he had to do. You know he would be here for you. There has been a breakdown in some machinery. Please forgive me." We could see that he was quite disturbed.

Giulio stepped toward Jim, patted him on the back, and said, "Don't make any excuses for me, Mr. Jim. Perhaps I can be of help in some way when I get to the ranch. I understand because I lived on a ranch for many summers when I grew up in Australia. I was an errand boy, a ranch hand, and a cowboy."

## Going Home to Teach School

We all laughed, and that broke the ice. I just waved at everyone. I wasn't able to take the time to make any introductions. Jim apologized to everyone as he was leaving the train platform, saying, "We need to take care of something." I had no idea what he was talking about. As we were walking down the street, we saw the two-tiered farm wagon loaded to overflowing. I couldn't believe my eyes. Giulio was smiling, jovial, and expressing keen boyish delight with what he saw. His kindness calmed my fears, and I was really learning to love this man more and more with his expression and understanding qualities. He was observing everyone around him.

There were two seats on the top. Jim helped me up to the back seat. Then he turned to help the count climb up to sit next to me. Then Giulio asked Jim, "Would you mind if I drive the horses? I drove this kind of conveyance in Australia."

"Okay, your highness. I'll sit up here with you, and Dotty is alright in the back." I was hanging over Giulio's shoulder when Giulio started the horses. The team seemed to know that they had a new driver. They did not seem to mind the heavy load and started to step ahead very slowly.

Jim carried on a bit of conversation with us, then he started to sing, "Oh bury me out on the lone prairie." Jim had a very nice voice; even the horses started to sway in their trotting. The singing amused Giulio, so he joined in. Finally, he was singing folk songs from Italy and France. It was enjoyable.

For conversation, we chatted about the type of people who have settled in North Dakota: immigrants and many nationalities from other countries who came in covered wagons and on the train from East and West.

We covered the seven miles to the ranch rather quickly, it seemed, considering the heavy load and crowded seating. We were not able to take the wagon into the barn, so Mother and Father dropped what they were doing and came to welcome us outside. It was a very touching welcome. Father gripped Giulio's hands with a very heartfelt understanding.

The count next bent over Mother and kissed her hand and then put one arm around her shoulder and said, "You are petite. My own mother is just about your size and smiles like you. All of my family calls her 'Mammina Lugie' or 'Aunt Lugie.' Her name is Louise."

The count cast his eyes all around and shook his head with approval. "Yes, this looks very much like home to me—like my uncle's ranch in Australia. You have the same type of house: all *L*s and the same long sheep sheds, nice high windmill, and long watering trough. They did not need as much hay as you have—many haystacks."

We were all pleased to see him adapt himself to the inconveniences of our prairie home and the enjoyment he took in doing things for himself. He followed Father and the men around outside, and he tried to help with every chore. The dogs followed him with wonderment.

Mother had arranged my room for the count; it opened off the living room. There was no door for privacy, but there were heavy red-velvet drapes covering the opening, which assured is privacy. I took Maple's little room off the kitchen, which was also our sewing room. Mother and Father had the last wing that was built, which was big enough for two rooms.

Our kitchen and dining room were together. That evening after supper we were all sitting at the table chatting when Mother and I began to clear the table. Father said, "Jim is going to look after all the chores tonight, so, Giulio, would you like to come with me into the other room, and we'll get out of the women's way?"

They went into the other room and closed the door. Soon after, Father came out and said: "Annie, we want you to come in here with us; we have something important to talk about." Father gave me a little wink as he turned to escort Mother into the room with Giulio. I had an idea what they would be discussing and wished Maple were there with me to help me curb my anxiety.

## Going Home to Teach School

Later, with elaborate gestures, Father gave me a full account of their talk. I listened as he described how the count started to talk with a little stammering and hesitation in order to speak every word cautiously. "As you know, I have come halfway across the United States to ask you for your daughter's hand in marriage. Will you trust me with her complete care? I love her very much, and I will cherish her."

Father said that he couldn't listen to the count explaining with such a shy look on his face; so he interrupted and said, "My dear count, my wife and I both appreciate your coming out here to ask for Dorothy's hand in marriage. It is such a heartfelt thing to do, and it makes her separation much easier for us. We realize that you will take her far away. As Americans, we give our children great freedom. We tell them that they must choose their own future and 'grow wings.' We knew this day would come."

Father continued, "My other daughter, Maple, and her fiancé just wrote to us and told us that they were married. They asked for our blessing. We only knew him as a little boy, so we don't know if we like him, but as long as they are happy, I give you my consent." He then turned to Mother and said, "As for my wife, Mrs. Berry, she can speak for herself."

And Mother said, "My dear count, I am very happy that you are my Dorothy's choice. I know that you are older than she is, and I think that is very good. Dorothy has not really grown up in many ways. She has told me that she loves you and admires you very much, and that is most important. You have my consent. Now you must ask our daughter."

Father took the floor again: "In these United States, we are very broadminded and all out for freedom. I always told my girls, 'When you fall in love, marry to suit your choice; no matter if we are satisfied or not.' But now we are all satisfied and happy." Father and Mother both had big smiles on their faces.

Giulio explained to them that he was a nobleman's son and came of age to acquire his share of the title, which is rightfully his own. He explained that he could not fill the positions in Italy offered to noblemen because of his eyesight—he was very nearsighted—so he held this position with the Italian steamship company and would need to live in both countries, Italy and the United States. He was not a wealthy man but had a comfortable income.

He explained to Father that his mother now held the title of "countess," and I would be "*la contessina*," meaning the "young countess," as long as his mother was living. Giulio further explained, "We all have to live by the laws of nobility; it is not difficult."

Father laughingly explained to Giulio, "There is no dowry going with my girls. I am not that wealthy. I wish I were so that I could send them with a 'purse.'" Both Father and Giulio laughed and shook hands.

This interview broke the ice and gave us a nice understanding all around. It was decided that I would go on with my school teaching as planned. The count would stay in New York City since there was a promotion coming for him. We would be married later. As Father said, "God will take care of our future; we trust Him implicitly for guiding and planning our lives." We were very happy to know that Giulio's parents were very broad in their religious teachings and had not let any sect sway them. Now this was the strongest bond that held us: our dedication to God and knowing that it reached into both of our families. No church or ecclesiastical power could sway us. In the understanding that we are God's children and he is our real father, this was the seal of our love for each other.

During this week that our nobleman visited us, we had many distracting things happen on our ranch. Many visitors and curiosity seekers came out to the ranch. Some were turned away; most all of our friends came to meet our distinguished visitor. One of our very closest friends came all the way from Virginia. They had money and position and came driving into our enclosure in their new Buick. They explained that they heard of our Italian count visiting us and wanted to ask about him. They wanted to be sure that he wasn't an imposter. Father assured the couple that the count was who he said he was and ready to meet any of our friends at any time. Father proved that he was from northern Italy with all the papers and credentials to prove it. Giulio could be traced back to the seventeenth century. He had his coat of arms, and the old castle was still standing at the foothills of the Alps.

Just as Father was explaining this, a Model-A Ford bounced into our ranch enclosure. These were friends of ours we hadn't seen in years who also wanted to be sure that this count wasn't an imposter. Mother and I looked out of the window to see who these people were and knew that they had to come in. So Mother went out to greet them and invite them in. I went to Giulio and put my arm around him and whispered, "These are people my parents will want you to get to know."

He smiled and said, "That is okay with me."

Then Father added, "Mark my word, Giulio, I'm going to buy a Model-A Ford real soon. I'm not giving up my buggy and my horses, but it sure would be a hoot, don't you think?"

Father and Mother ushered our friends into the house, and with cheerful voices said, "Count Giulio, here are some of our best and closest friends. They have come to meet you and Dorothy."

I led Giulio forward and waved to all of them. "My dear friends, this is Count Giulio. I will ask him to pronounce his complete name, since it is very difficult for us to pronounce."

Giulio was just as I expected: he was happy to meet our friends in his own way. He stepped forward, clicked his heels together, and bent low over the hand of the ladies, smiled at the gentlemen, and pronounced his complete name.

"I am Count Giulio de Sauteiron St. Clement, and in Italy I would have to add, de Berthamond to my name."

We were all seated, and the conversation was jovial and interesting. Giulio appeared very comfortable with our friends. Mother served lemonade and cookies. Our guests left quite convinced that our visitor was a bona fide count. Other visitors came out of curiosity, but Jim would politely answer their questions and then with diplomacy ask them to leave, explaining that the family had enough company for one day. A reporter for news in general said that he heard that this was a "scoop story," but Jim assured him that the story had already been given to the newspapers.

The many chores to be done around the ranch were most enjoyable to all of us. Giulio loved the animals and was so pleased to go with me to visit all of them. We would make the rounds in the evening when they were all in their places. Father's way of judging character was to watch his animals' reactions. He could tell if the animals were upset or showed fear. Father would have no business transactions with anyone who caused any stress for them. He had proven this many times. Most often the animals would just look up to see who was around and go back to their grazing or resting.

Giulio and I went on horseback for errands to bring in the cattle and the horses into the barn. We'd ride with Jim to cut out a horse, cow, or sheep or to take lunches to the outside ranch hands. We also picked choke cherries from the bushes by riding through the gullies. When we returned from berry picking, we would sit on the front porch to have a plate lunch or just talk.

One day a neighbor rider dashed into the enclosure and yelled, "Where's Abie?"

I answered, "With the haying crew!"

"There is a prairie fire on Knife River Flats!"

Mother ran for the ram's horn and blew a warning blast. This brought Father, Jim, and all the crews, and even the neighbors heard it. Prairies were our worst enemy. In jig time our men had gathered all the firefighting apparatuses and had put them in the lumber wagon and dashed off to the flats. I hitched the horse team

## Going Home to Teach School

to the buckboard, while Giulio got the gunnysacks and brooms; then we rode off to the flats. When we arrived, everyone there was just getting the fire under control; they had stopped the wide sweep of flames. Giulio and I helped by dragging a wet sack to smolder the grass and watch for little flames that might start springing up again. Father had his crew go back to the ranch, and he brought us back home in the buckboard after we finished. Father and the crew were really pleased to see Giulio helping and his quick action in wiping out another new flame that had started.

We found out that a cigarette stub was thrown down on the road, which started a flame on a patch of dry grass and nearby tumbleweed. One of the neighbors caught the fellow who tossed the cigarette, took him into Taylor, and had him put in the jail. He would have to work to pay for the lost hay.

The prairie fire brought under control helped us to get to know Giulio more. He was quick to help all of us and felt quite pleased to be able to as well.

Visitors were still coming to the ranch to meet or see "the nobleman from Italy." Father would meet them and say, "Yes, we have a nobleman here, but he is not on exhibition, boys! He came here to rest, and by Jiminy Crickets, I'm going to let him rest."

One cowboy came all the way from Medora, asking to meet the Italian nobleman. He said that he had worked for the Marquis de Mores in Medora, and that he was the kindest and mot refined gentleman he had ever met. He said that he taught him how to wait on the marquis and his lady in the European manner. Father ushered him in to meet Giulio. It turned out that Giulio was very much impressed with the story and the manners of the man who worked closely with the dashing French marquis. After the gentleman left, we prepared to leave for the "Old Settlers Picnic." This picnic was given every year for the citizens of Taylor and for the farmers and ranchers. Father and Mother could not leave the ranch, so Giulio and I hitched up the ponies again to the wagon. They jogged along so nicely and quite fast too with their swinging gait. We took some homemade food with us: our canned cherry pie, cookies, and a loaf of bran homemade bread. Everything we did seemed to be more enjoyable. Giulio drove the team as they jogged along, passing other wagons and carriages, even our friends with the Buick and Old Model-A Ford. I was glad it didn't give our team any ideas of racing. There were about two hundred people at the picnic. The food was all laid out on plank tables, and everyone helped themselves. The aroma was appetizing and very tempting. Almost everyone had heard by now that an Italian nobleman was visiting the A-BAR-B Ranch. Then the word went around that "Dotty is not going to get married yet because she has promised to teach the Jesperson School."

When we arrived, I felt so proud to be on the arm of my nobleman. Walrus Wiggins was the master of ceremonies, but he called himself the "boss of the shindig." He claimed to have the "biggest mouth" in Stark County.

Those who had met Giulio rushed over to say hello, then asked Walrus to announce from the platform that we had a distinguished visitor there. Then surprisingly, Walrus asked if I would do the announcing. So Walrus said over the microphone, "I think Dotty can do this introduction best."

I was reluctant to do this but was given no choice in front of all my friends. So I stepped up on the platform with my knees a bit weak and my voice a bit soft and said, "I am very pleased to introduce to you Count Giulio de Sauteiron de St. Clement of Italy and New York City." Giulio could see I was a little nervous, so he stepped up on the platform and held onto my arm. He bowed and gave everyone a gracious smile. He whispered in my ear and said that I pronounced his name perfectly. I think that was one of the reasons why I was so nervous, and his reassurance made me feel like a real lady.

## Going Home to Teach School

Then Walrus came forward and said, "Give them both a big hand, Dorothy Berry and this Italian nobleman." I didn't think Walrus could pronounce the long Italian name; I thought wrong. The response and the applause were deafening. Walrus came forward again. "How about another big hand for our friends who are engaged to be married."

Then a voice out of the crowd yelled and laughed, "She can't get married. She is going to teach school."

Now everyone was talking and asking questions. So we had to tell our story to everyone. It was getting to be a day to remember. Afterward, Giulio was asked if he was having a good time. He said, "Oh yes, this is quite a picnic." Then to my surprise, they actually made him one of the judges for the games. It was rather fun to observe; then I actually took part in one of the games—the potato race. We left in the wee small hours of the morning, and at daybreak we drove into the ranch enclosure. The dogs didn't bark—just lots of tail wags to greet us. Giulio did not treat me like a sweetheart, just like a very attentive friend and in a very considerate manner. He said that was the Italian way.

Everyone on the A-BAR-B Ranch understood the one unwritten law: this is no place for any lazy bones. Everyone was up unusually early this last day of Giulio's visit. From my window I could see the men at their chores; the haying crew was in the bunkhouse for breakfast.

Giulio was following Father around, and both were talking with their hands. I joined them to call them in for breakfast. We were all in a jovial mood to hide the sadness we felt, knowing that he would be leaving us.

As we sat around the breakfast table, Father said, "Just listen, the air is filled with animal voices, nonsensical chatter like women over their household chores or over their children."

"Those animals are talking about me" Giulio said. "I understand animal voices too; they're talking about my leaving." We all laughed and agreed. Giulio continued, "They are saying that the big visitor is leaving so we will now get more attention." Then the horses started making sounds.

Mother said, "Those whinnies tell a nice story. They wish you lived here, and they would have a lot of nice rides and drives and show you new places." Then we all laughed with Mother at such a clever comment.

Giulio and I went in the living room and had our last visit together. He held me in his arms and said nice things, mostly in Italian, but I seemed to understand. He said, "Just teach the one term of school." He smiled and then kissed my hand. Father took us to Taylor in the red-wheeled buggy drawn by our team Baxter and Bixby. He made them hurry along, and we arrived at the Taylor train station in the nick of time.

Giulio waved to all the bystanders. We had said our sweet good-bye at the ranch, so he shook Father's hand and said good-bye to me and stepped on the train as it moved away. It gained momentum and whisked around the bend and disappeared from sight. The cowboys standing around began to sing: "I saw the train go 'round the bend, good-bye, my lover, good-bye." And they looked at me as they sang. I smiled at them and tried to hide my feelings. Father and I walked to the country store and got our mail, and Father did some trading. We did not start a conversation with anyone. We didn't comment on the weather or what we would be doing tomorrow.

## Dotty Starts Teaching at Jesperson

Now my school days started. Dear old golden rule days in a prairie school house, bordering on the Jesperson farm, about five miles south of Taylor. I had thirty pupils enrolled, but I only had ten of the smallest children to start. This was a farming neighborhood, and the older children had to help with outside work. I wanted this school because it was near home, in a nice neighborhood, and had nice buildings. I was told this was a tough school for a lady teacher. The kids wanted learning but they were big, overgrown boys who didn't want to be hampered by rules or sit too long in cramped seats behind desks. They didn't mean to be unruly, but it took the firm hand of the male sex to keep decorum.

Father had a strong influence with the school board, and he had hired teachers for the Taylor school, so he explained to them, "Give my daughter, Dorothy, a chance at this school. She knows all the people, and she is right out of college and has big ideas and notions. She wants to try to help these boys to learn what is most important. She has a way with young'uns in coaxing them along without using brawn or hand-power persuasion. She'll appeal to their pride. If she isn't able to handle them, then turn them over to Schoolmaster Jenner, the champion athlete of Stark County. That's all fair and square. Please give Dorothy a chance."

The school board decided to give me the school, and the school superintendent informed me, "The school is yours, Miss Berry. We think that this is the right place for a beginning teacher. Your softhearted feminine qualities should react on those oversmart cowpunchers. We'll help you get them graded and started."

Another reason I wanted the school was that it paid forty dollars a month instead of thirty-five dollars. I was informed that there was no money in the treasury for the schools at present. I would receive a warrant that would draw 6 percent interest until the county money came in.

Father and Mother were very pleased and happy about my school. "Keep your salary for that 'dowry money' you hear about in Italy. Anyway, you will have a little nest egg, and the count said that his American money makes him independent and happy."

The school house stood on a main traveled road to Taylor. It was the typical long lumber building with a peaked roof and a chimney. It was painted white with yellow trim. There were three windows on each side and a doorway in front. This led into a vestibule, and all conveniences were provided. There was a closet to hang the clothes and a place below for shoes and rubbers.

A long bench held a water pail and a dipper, two wash basins, and a soap dish. Clean towels were provided by the mothers. The long schoolroom had two rows of desks and seats. My desk and swivel chair stood in front near the entrance. Blackboards lined both sides of the room, and a potbellied stove stood in front of them. Outside, there were two little privies standing back and some distance apart. One was marked "boys," and other was marked "girls." There were no locks on these doors, but each had a hook and staple. There were boxes built in that held issue paper and the usual catalogs of Montgomery Ward and Company or a Sears and Roebuck of a past date.

In front of the door were two hitching posts to tie the horses. What more could a school teacher ask for on the Western prairies? The first Monday in September I came to school on a Monday. Fifteen children were waiting for me, all clean and neatly dressed, and some had smiling faces, and some looked a little scared, or in doubt.

Two boys, about fourteen, as tall as myself, drawled out a greeting. I overheard this from one: "She's easy. If she's going to stick to rules, we'll throw her out the window." They sauntered in and slouched in the adjoining seats. The whole morning was occupied in getting adjusted and finding the right seating arrangement. The superintendent of schools would visit us and compare us with the graded schools.

Through lunch and recess time, we all got better acquainted. A few of the children I had met had visited our A-BAR-B Ranch with their parents. I asked the two boys who made the remarks to stay a moment after school so we could talk. I put my hands on their shoulders and said "Boys, don't throw me out of the window. You could do it easy, I know. If you are not satisfied or if I can't have discipline, I will gladly change schools with Mr. Jenner."

## Going Home to Teach School

They stammered and scuffed, "We were just fooling, and we really like you." Their faces were real sweet and beaming; as we ended our chat, we shook hands.

I never seemed to have all of my thirty pupils at any one time. The older ones had to stay at home to help with the farm work, so I never complained. This settlement was entirely made up of Norwegians and Swedes. They were thrifty, honest people of the Lutheran religion. They had their own church and minister in Taylor, and they brought up their children with a deep reverence for God and his word.

Every family seemed to have from six to ten children, and they had roomy, spreading farmhouses and very large barns and good accommodating sheds. They took keen interest in their farm animals, just as we did on the A-BAR-B.

In this neighborhood, every family took turns to board the teacher two weeks at a time. I liked the idea of living in every home, so I conformed to every arrangement. I would stay all week and go home on Friday night. I would ride my bicycle if it was not windy. If the wind was too strong, I could always borrow a pony. I was at home with every family. I soon found out that I had another job besides teaching. In my domestic course at the North Dakota Agricultural College, I took sewing. I would make my own dresses and Sunday dresses. I could make my own patterns or buy them. My board came to four dollars a week, and usually my sewing bill was $.00. Mother said that my bookkeeping was just like my Father's. I only had to put down zeros every week.

Every Friday afternoon the school would give me a program. There was talent in this school, and this was an opportunity to express it. We had violins, fiddles, mouth organs, and a zither. All of the children had good voices for solos, or they would be in a chorus. We would have recitations and little skits. We invited the parents and any outsiders. We would sometimes serve refreshments; either the children would, or I did by myself.

A sign on the roadway read, "Public Program at Jesperson School." Several of these Friday programs stand out in my memory. One Friday my little round-faced Johnny got up to surprise me. He did not memorize very well, but he stumbled along.

He said, "Day is done, and the darkness falls from the wings of night." (I was saying to myself, "As a feather is wafted downward from an eagle in its flight.")

Sister Edith stood near him, and Johnny was looking toward her and begging for help "As...as...as," Edith was making signs and forming the word with her mouth. Finally, she said aloud but with a soft whisper. "Think, Johnny, think. What does a bird drop when he flies?"

Before Johnny could think, there were loud guffaws. Then everyone in the whole room was laughing hysterically. There were spasms of laughter as I raised my voice to say, "School is dismissed!" Then all the children flocked out of school laughing as they jumped on their horses and rode away. The incident circulated all around town till the whole town was laughing over what happened in school that day.

One outstanding experience happened while teaching school on the coldest day of the year. It was in January, and I was boarding at the Jesperson home. We had gone through cold weather before, and some blizzards had kept us away from the schoolhouse. This day it was clear and cold, and the morning sun made rainbows on the ice-covered prairies. The house was warm with two stoves burning wood to full capacity and shining red through the grates.

Mr. Jesperson came in the house with his two big boys and informed us, "No school today, Miss Berry. It is fifty below zero, and even the air is cracking up. The animals won't go out, and they are eating inside." I was walking the floor and looking out of the windows on each side.

Suddenly I stopped and looked at the schoolhouse in the distance. "There is school today. There is someone over there. Smoke is coming out of the chimney. I must go. Those children must have school. I've been out in forty below zero, so I think I can make it over there."

They all agreed with me; then came the bundling up with warm clothes. I dressed up the two youngest children and then myself. We looked like three Eskimos wrapped in fur from head to foot. We had hooded parkas with wool scarves over our faces. In our pockets we had hot bricks, and we each carried a lunch box.

It wasn't too bad walking over the ice-frozen snow, to hear the crunch and the musical sound of each step. We would watch our breath floating out like smoke. Mr. Jesperson had warned us as we left; "Don't talk or laugh, or your faces will freeze that way." We walked quietly along, not even looking at each other but with our eyes were fixed on the smoke coming from our schoolhouse chimney.

When we arrived, we were greeted by Knute, our nearest neighbor. He had brought four of his children, two boys and two girls, to the school. We all worked together to put the desks around the stove so that we could huddle together. Our school was in session. Knute contented himself with magazines. I gave special attention to each child, and we cleared up some hard problems. It was a successful morning. We stopped at noon and had our lunch. I made hot tea for everyone. Our little tea kettle danced and sang a tune. The stove was red, so the children made up a song about it: "The stove's potbelly is red as can be, red as can be. 'Cuz it don't know it's five below; it's fifty below outside."

After that we did not feel like studying. So the children all sang their school songs and Norwegian songs. At two o'clock, Knute decided it was best to go home. It was not a blizzard after all but just clear cold, and it had gone up to forty degrees below zero. Knute wrapped his children in blankets in the wagon. The horses had stood in the outside shed, so they were warm. Then I bundled the two Jesperson children in their furs and ushered them across the frozen snow to the Jesperson home. We had a good day after all.

The last Friday in June my school closed, and it was a gala day for the whole neighborhood. Parents and friends were invited. Even the farm work couldn't keep them away. The children arrived in fluffy dresses and slick cowboy outfits with gay-colored neckerchiefs. I wore a blue party dress that I had worn at college. Everyone was in a festive mood.

There were no classes, and everyone was on the program. It was their own arrangement, and it looked quite professional. There was a violin solo, a short play, a ladies' sewing bee, fiddle solo of "Turkey in the Straw," and several recitations, both serious and comical. Then the main attraction was the "Beauty Machine," which was a performance of three ugly, scary witches who came in by the front entrance, walked through a long curtained machine, and came out the other end looking like three bewitching beauties. It was quite an attraction and got many laughs. After that, there were more fiddle solos: "Arkansas Traveler" and "March of the Sugar Bowl." The children entertained us when they sang songs from their music books.

After the program we had lemonade and cookies for everyone. There were little bags of candy and peanuts for the children to take home. There were a few awards passed around for: best speller, best reader, best attendance, best observer, and even for helping with farm work. There was a happy good-bye to all for the end of the school-year program. It was understood that I would return to teach for the next term.

It was wonderful to be back on the A-BAR-B Ranch and my big animal family. Father was singing some new songs: words he had learned from the newspapers, but the tunes were just the same, only different words. One of our rancher friends was running his own ranch in the Badlands. He would visit us occasionally and would always come over if we needed him. We shared working crews with nearby farmers and ranchers. He was interested to know that Father was selling his foundation stock. Father's bookkeeping was in arrears, and Mother was making sure there were no losses. I would have helped, but I couldn't juggle figures. My expertise was writing poetry.

Father bought a Model-A Ford that summer for the ranch *[1903]*. It was affectionately called the "Fordmobile" and was the first vehicle mass-produced by the Henry Ford Motor Company. It could chug-chug along the two-track rutted roads and save horseflesh. It was built to run on two cylinders at eight horsepower that could reach thirty miles per hour. Father wouldn't drive it that fast though. One of the rules was that no one was allowed to go out alone without a mechanic along. Not one of us on the ranch could back up or turn around on a fifty-cent piece like the car agent did. We all turned around in a circle and took a lot of room doing it. Father had a gas tank put up on the ranch so we would have plenty of "juice" when we wanted to go in a hurry. Mother was the only one who would not even try to drive it.

## Letters from Will and Maple Frost

Maple's letters were always exciting, Father said. "She keeps me sitting on a tinderbox." Now she said: "We think we're going to have a baby; the doctor is not sure." Father asked Dr Stickney, and he grunted. Mother said that was professional courtesy; doctors won't give each other away. Other letters followed, and finally we read: "We are going to have a baby."

Out of a clear sky came a most surprising letter from Dayton, Ohio, in Maple's handwriting. Mother read it aloud:

> Dear Folkses in House and Barns
> We have moved and everything we own is in a nice six-room cottage. It has happened so quickly and we are very happy. My Bill has a top brass job as

Manager in a big typewriter business. He came well recommended because of his high marks in Business College. His record was, "The Speediest Typist." His hours are good and he is manager over a Division. They are figuring out his top salary right now. The baby is fine, but so active. He wants to come out before his time. We know it is a boy because no girl would act like this. He will be here in August. I want you, Mother, or Dotty to come here at that time. We will buy your ticket.

Love from Maple and Will

    We were all delighted over Maple's news. I was hoping Mother would go to Dayton but always felt she was needed more at home. So it all pointed for me to go to Dayton before returning to school. On my first week of vacation I had to join May Hayes and attend the "Teacher's Institute" in Dickinson. May and I had grown up a lot since teaching school and holding a responsible position. We were really women now. Both of us were looking forward to marriage in the near future. There was so much happening in this month of August.

    I was ready to go to Dayton, Ohio. I cashed in one of my interest-drawing school warrants and again went through the trip to Taylor. There was always the curiosity of the Taylorites. I took the afternoon train to Chicago and on to Dayton to help my sister, Maple, with the overly active baby to arrive. My new brother-in-law, William Frost, met me at the station and took me to their honeymoon cottage. There was Maple, a little fat girl, just one size all over. As I looked at her, I wondered how she could have possibly managed to do all the work required with moving into the cottage.

    We were like two little girls in Maple's home, making doll clothes. We would lay all the little clothes that we had made out on their bed for Bill to see when he came home from his office. We raved about them, and he would look so bashful. I was always watching Maple to see if I saw anything unusual. If so, then I would grab the phone and call the doctor. Her doctor did not have the patience like our Dr. Stickney. He would actually be annoyed and say, "You tend to your knitting. Babies don't come into the world so fast and without some warning. I'm watching. And I'll be there when the baby comes."

The baby chose a very convenient time to arrive. He came on a Sunday at ten o'clock in the morning. He also gave enough warning, so we were all at our posts. The doctor and nurse were with Maple, and her bed had already been specially prepared for her. Will and I were fluttering around like two uncaged birds. When an order was given, we would bump into each other in our hurry to help. I thought they needed hot water, so I brought in a tea kettle of boiling water. No one scolded me, but they did laugh.

Even the doctor made a pun to break the tension: "This is a very hot August morning, but it will be cooler very soon because we are going to have a little Frost!" We all laughed, and we laughed some more. Maple laughed so very hard that she forgot her pains. Then little Melvin slid right out into this world.

It was a rapturous moment. Maple called out, "Oh, God, my baby!"

The doctor and nurse were very busy taking care of Maple. The nurse wrapped the baby in a soft towel and handed him to me and said, "Take him into the other room and lay him on the bed. Be sure to lay him on his stomach. Keep the towel loose around him and see that his head is free so he can breathe."

It was the sweetest responsibility I ever had in my whole life. That little newborn baby raised his head, his little eyes opened, and he looked right at me. He was making grimaces at me. I was sure he smiled at me. Then he seemed conscious of his whole little body since he was quivering. I told all this to the nurse, but she did not respond. I supposed that she was so used to newborn babies, it did not register as anything unusual.

This was a joyous household; everything centered on baby Melvin. We would notice some slight change or growth every twenty-four hours. Letters from the A-BAR-B Ranch showed us they were just as elated. Father was still twittering with his cigars, even though he never smoked them.

Count Giulio was in Chicago, and he planned to come to Dayton for a Saturday and a Sunday when I was ready to go home. But all plans worked out beautifully, and he spent the two days with us. Watching Melvin was our greatest enjoyment. Maple and Will liked him very much, and he gave us a very vivid picture of his life as a nobleman. He taught us what was required of a royal family in Italy. His great misfortune was his eyesight. He was very nearsighted, so he could not hold any of the positions offered in the army or navy. He said that it was through prayers and faith in God that he was given his present position in the United States. Then he added: "It was God's will to bring Dorothy and me together." He continued, "Now we will plan our lives together." There was a strong bond of love that bridged our different countries and nationalities.

Giulio-Dorothy-Maple holding baby Melvin-William Frost -1903 in Dayton Ohio

## Going Home to Teach School

The next day Count Giulio and I boarded a train for Chicago, and there we parted. My Giulio for New York City, and I, for St. Paul and on to Taylor, North Dakota. My visit to Dayton was like a dream. But I was happy to be back to my prairie with its black-rooted buffalo grass and its thick green sage that stretched from the horizon lines all around.

My head was in the clouds as I walked around trying to help with the chores. I made some new dresses for my trousseau. I sent an order to Montgomery Ward and Company for many things that were advertised for what every bride should have. I wanted to sing, but I couldn't since I was tone deaf, just like Father. So I developed a sort of tuneless ditty and made up my own rhymes just like he did. The animals liked it. Mother would say, "I can't say I like such singing, but it is convenient since I always know where Abie and Dotty are."

The summer was passing quickly. I visited May in Dickinson, and I attended several harvest dances around the country. We had some company on the ranch. Almost every day there was a birthday party at the A-BAR-B. Queenie, our pet cow had a calf. A colt was born in the pasture. One of the ranch hands put up a flag to let Father know where the calf was. That is how we came to name her Banner. The next day our prize pig "Juliette" had another litter of Poland-China hogs. I felt sure that the ranch crew would help with the litter. I thought to myself "not me"; I won't be helping with the piglets. I will soon be "Countess Dorothy," but then I did not voice my thoughts to anyone; I just got to work.

Father remarked: "I am a bit tired of being midwife with every newborn animal. I always heard that animals could take care of themselves."

"They can," I said, "but you've got that little black instrument case, and everything alive on this ranch knows it." Mother was laughing as I said it. Then I chimed in again, "Our ranch is so different from all the ranches I visit. Our ranch is so human that the animals are humanized. We can't change the order now, Father; we'll have to go on and baby the stock, and we love it."

We had a phonograph that brought us some of the New York song hits. We also had quite a few records of the Western cowboy songs. It was fun to hear our ranch hands sing along with the records as we played them on the phonograph. Some evenings we would have song fests. It really was a good time to relax and enjoy the company of our hard-working cowboys and get to hear their voices.

Giulio's letters that we wrote to each other were passing back and forth very quickly. The postmaster in Taylor would inform everyone who asked about us; but they would respond by saying, "She has promised that she would teach at the Jesperson School again, even if she has a castle waiting for her over in Italy."

Then they would ask me, "Hey, Dorothy, are you going to get married, or are you going to teach school?"

I tried to use my Father's tactics because he always gave an answer that told nothing but would lead them on so they would draw their own conclusions. My answer was, "I'm going to be a *real old maid* school teacher." Then I just smiled and chuckled at myself. That is probably what I would be if I hadn't been blessed to have met Giulio, my Italian prince. I guess I won't be a Cinderella or an old maid. Then I chuckled to myself again.

September rolled around, and I was back in the Jesperson School. I always loved teaching, and I learned to love that old school. I was pleasantly surprised when I walked in the first day to see how good it looked. The janitors and school helpers must have spent some quality time at the school at the end of August because it was all fresh-smelling and clean with some new arrangements: pictures on the walls, new potted plants, and a flower vase with flowers on my desk. It was such a welcome sight. It made me wonder how I could ever leave here when I would be leaving for Italy to be married. I had no idea when. I would have to be patient and just love every minute of my time here making memories. That was how I had to look at it: only think about what is important today and enjoy every minute of it. We can't have our head in the clouds looking for tomorrow to come. We have to make each day count. Father used to say, "Why put off until tomorrow what you can be doing today? We have too much to do today to be wasting the precious time God has given us to do His work today. He'll take care of tomorrow when it gets here."

After teaching class and walking back to my room at the boarding house, I thought of Giulio's sweet little mother, who was now corresponding with me. She welcomed questions that I had for her, and she would enlighten me on anything I wanted to know. I was learning how to read and write in Italian, and she was struggling to learn English. I wrote about wearing formals for state occasions. She wrote back and suggested that I have two formals and just some plain basic dresses. So I bought a Butterick's pattern and made the formals and some basic dresses for myself. I ordered the fabric through our country store in Taylor: white and garnet of heavy satin.

I was happy in my school work all week and thankful to have good boarding at the different homes. I was sewing for the families during the week nights and then doing the sewing of my own dresses on the weekends, sometimes sewing into the nights and sitting on a comfy settee next to a kerosene lamp. I made everything by hand: first basting with a good quality thread, then finishing off with a short, tight stitch and a hem stitch.

Father finally sold our prize pig, Juliette, because she was getting very cross and jealous of her own children and would punish them. Father said that he was afraid she would end up in a sausage real soon. She served her purpose of birthing many piglets over the last couple of years. She certainly was worth her salt, he would say.

Well now, of all the well-laid plans of mice and men, the A-BAR-B had one of its biggest surprises. Count Giulio wrote in his most recent letter that he was commissioned to sail to Italy this month of January. He asked if I would join him and be married here in Taylor before we sail.

There was no alternative now since I had promised I would go with him when his call came in. And now, the call had come. So I made a call too! I gave up my teaching school, and changes were made in surrounding schools so Mr. Jenner could take over the Jesperson School for me.

I made the last day a gala day to say good-bye to the children and their parents. We repeated some of our best skits, and the little fiddlers did their very best, even to a square dance. We all took part and in the dancing and singing and even made refreshments for the occasion; cupcakes and donuts were made by the mothers. They also provided hot coffee and hot chocolate. Then I had the sweetest surprise from my dear students. They presented me with a piece of luggage. And it was a very nice pigskin traveling bag. With my nervous sense of humor, I thought to myself, *This couldn't be Juliette, could it?* Then of course, I knew it wasn't, but I could refer to my traveling bag as my "Juliette bag." But that would have to be my secret.

Our farewell greetings were very sincere and very profuse. There were tears in my eyes, and some of the children cried. They hugged me and asked when would I be back. The children knew that I was marrying an Italian nobleman, and that I would become a countess. Would I wear a tiara? How would I dress for royalty? I realized that all those things had been talked over in their homes, so I tried to explain that these were modern times. I was going to dress and live my own life. I would only wear a tiara for very big public occasions. I would live in the castle sometimes, and I would also live in a modern home in Rome. I expected to come back to the United States every two years. I promised that I would come back to North Dakota for visits. Then I said good-bye to my school, and I was heading back to the A-BAR-B Ranch.

## Going Home to Teach School

Everything was done so hurriedly, and again I went through the ritual: a big good-bye demonstration of farewell to all the animals. That was a sensitive moment for me; I smiled through my tears as I stroked each one. I could never forget what each one gave to me—their trust and their love.

Both Father and Mother took me to Taylor in a sled drawn by Baxter and Bixby, our forever faithful team. The air was crisp and cold. The prairie dew on the land sparkled like diamonds. The sky was deep blue with swift-moving fleece-like clouds. Father kept the conversation in a silly vein, coaching me about what my formal manners would be like. "Don't use Western phrases or Western slang or walk with a slouch! Just remember that your Father belongs to that royal order of knighthood. He is an esquire, and I am lord and master of two thousand acres, known as the A-BAR-B Ranch! You can tell them we raise only thoroughbreds of the highest intelligence." Father kept our spirits up, and we parted smiling. I waved to all the bystanders as they waved to me with mouth-open awe. My quick decision and my hurried leaving on an eastbound train were too mysterious for them to grasp the real reason. It was more like a fairy tale—like something you'd read about happening to someone else: not quite real but wanting it to be. And I knew that I was living it. It wasn't a fairy tale; it was better than a storybook, imaginary tale. It was real, and it was happening to me.

After I left Father and Mother, I went into the Lewis L. Lewis Store and treated everyone to apple cider until the cider barrel ran dry. Then the news spread over a wide acreage. The news kept traveling and gaining new details as it went along. It wasn't just gossip; it was magical. The good folk of North Dakota were always inclusive. That was the life of the West, seeing the covered wagons come and go, and now it was the Northern Pacific railway taking people west and east and back again.

Father and Mother returned to the A-BAR-B, and Father said, "We've made a big mistake, Annie. We should have had more children to keep this ranch going. On these other ranches and farms, the kids marry and stay around home and look after their folks. Now think! Dotty is going across the Big Pond to live in Italy for two whole years. We're entirely alone now."

It was a sad thought, but I was too happy in new plans and a new life to realize the lonesomeness and sadness of the A-BAR-B.

*Chapter Thirteen -*
# Cowgirl to Countess

Count Giulio met me at the station, beaming and happy like a little boy, trying to tell me so much that he would forget his English and finish his sentences; either in Italian or French. And then he would laugh. How much he has changed from the first time we met. He was stiff and proper then and now much more like himself, I think. He is a happy man with a twinkle in his eye. He told me that he was living in a friend's home—the home of Doctor Mackey and his wife, Eloise, along with the wife's mother, Mrs. Ward. All of them were trying to help him with his marriage plans. Living in their home was quite unusual for him. He said he knew that he was starting to enjoy life as he never knew it before.

Mrs. Ward came forward with ideas and plans for the marriage ceremony in their home, if Giulio and I would look after obtaining the marriage license. Her minister was a Baptist. That might have been a problem, but Giulio quite agreed and said that we would be married by the Italian Council in New York City. Then Giulio laughingly said, "Our marriage now is going to be tied very tightly, Dorothy. We'll be married by a Baptist minister, and then when we arrive in Rome, our marriage will be sanctioned under the blessing of the pope. This is the custom for nobility.

*Pope Saint Pius X* was considered a pastoral pope, in the sense of encouraging personal holiness, piety, and reflected deep Christian values. Was there ever a wedding of nobility as sweet and simple as ours? We stood under a bower of flowers in Dr. Mackey's parlor, the Baptist minister tying the knot. Since it was a ring ceremony, Giulio slipped on my finger a plain band that he had purchased in a five-and-ten-cent store. The nobleman groom wore a navy-blue business suit. I wore my traveling suit of royal blue.

Giulio had a white flower in his button hole, and I held a small bridal bouquet. An Italian couple stood up with us. It was Giulio's closest friends from Italy. And the household stood with us also.

I wrote the whole description to the A-BAR-B Ranch. Somehow I knew that they were pleased with this mixed-up arrangement. Our wedding trip was just as unusual. It had to be Giulio's business trip and the only way for us to get back to New York City together. We spent two days in St. Louis and again on the train and then two more days in Buffalo, New York.

These were very hurried, busy days for Giulio, and I would busy and content myself in each city, sightseeing and shopping. We played and laughed and made a joke of our unusual honeymoon. We wrote funny letters to the A-BAR-B and also to Maple and Will in Dayton, Ohio. Our whole honeymoon was a sub-Rosa outside of the family and there was no publicity in the newspapers. Father took care of a formal account of a marriage of nobility, and that sufficed for our Western friends. Giulio and I were so entirely churchless people. I accepted my father's church: "Any place out in the open under the canopy of the sky from horizon line to horizon line with God's everlasting arms and close nearness." Father had said this when we had first moved out to our prairie ranch; and we had loved it so much.

We all said, "This is the church of the A-BAR-B Ranch."

## Board the Italian Ship to Rome, Italy

When we arrived in New York City, it seemed that everything was provided for us. The Italian liner was in port and reloading to sail. The *President Wilson* was a palace on the water. To me it was a fairyland beyond my wildest dreams. To Giulio, it was one of his many steamship homes as his work took him back and forth to Italy. I was considered a very good sailor. I was interested in this entirely new experience. Giulio had a pet name for me, "Seagob." That was my nickname for a long time.

When we arrived in Naples, I stepped foot on Italian soil. We had time for sightseeing before boarding our train for Rome. We visited the buried city of Pompeii and then Mount Vesuvius. It was hard to describe the reactions of a cowgirl to this ancient world. Giulio's explanation of everything made a lasting impression that I can relive over and over in my mind.

I loved the little mountebanks, the diving boys who would jump off the pier and bring up the silver pieces in their mouths. They wanted a twenty-five piece to do the trick. They would also dance and sing or show off by eating a full plate of macaroni and letting it slide down their throats.

The wind was just right for us to take the path around the crater of Mount Vesuvius and look down at the mass of what looked like boiling chocolate syrup. Our ride to Rome on a European train was surprising by making comparison to our US trains. We stepped in a compartment, and we were all by ourselves. We held each other close, and Giulio squeezed my hand and gave me a big kiss on my cheek. He was a gentleman, with truly a kind manner. We glanced out the window to enjoy the scenery along the way. It certainly gave me a vivid picture of the Italian countryside with such a rough and changeable terrain.

It was dark when we arrived in Rome. Giulio looked out of the window to see who may be waiting on the station platform. He waved and laughed, "They are all here to meet us, Dorothy, even dear little Mother." I looked out and waved at that dear little woman who resembled my own dear Mother at home on the ranch. I recognized his family from photos his mother had sent me. There was Giulio's oldest brother's widow, "Noble Donna Eugenia," and his first cousin Marquis Alfredo Dulec. These were the closest relatives of my dear Giulio, and my welcome was spontaneous and sincere.

They took us to the family house in Rome, and we had our first evening together in the Blue Room, and a supper was served.

It was warm and intimate, and I found out Giulio's pet name was "Snookie." I couldn't believe I had a pet name too; it was "Little Red Devil" because of my reddish-blond hair.

I was impressed with the house in Rome; it was a six-story building with a twelve-room apartment, a caretaker, a manager, and a janitor who lived on the first floor (considered a basement floor) with his family. There was also an elevator.

Giulio and I were to stay with Eugenia and Lugie, our little mother, while in Rome. Here was a modern home in every respect with a setting of the antique magnificence of an aristocratic family. There was a high stone wall around this home, with a locked gate. Inside were the gardens and modern garages, and all this stood quite near the Vatican.

I would pinch myself and then tell Giulio to pinch me. "Am I really here in Rome, Italy with all this grandeur?"

Giulio would pinch me and then hug me, "Yes, here is my little cowgirl from the prairies and now my *contessina nobile, cara piccina mia!*"

We walked all through the gardens in this enclosure and wondered how they could get so many different plants to grow with such luxury and abundance? Our garden on the A-BAR-B Ranch would spread over acres and not produce nearly as much, with its prairie grasses, tumbleweeds, and white gumbo soil.

Giulio would explain: "This is the secret of Italian determination. They only have this small peninsula, a volcanic eruption from the bottom of the sea. It is the richest soil, and they keep it rich organically, which does triple us in produce." This little country was indeed very rich.

We did not do any sightseeing in Rome at this time as we would be here for two years; so our first visit was to be in the Castle Berthamond in the Province of Piedmont, in the foothills of the Alps.

Giulio was like a little boy planning this trip. He said, "This is our real honeymoon, *viaggio.*" We were to go in the family car, a Fiat limousine. The family chauffeur, Renato, was a very good driver. He was proven to be dependable, loyal almost to a fault, with a real funny-bone sense of humor. We were riding through the most historical and picturesque part of Italy with its modern homes and old ruins almost side by side.

Giulio would point out everything of interest along the way. We would comment seriously, and then we would laugh together. Renato would talk to us through the tube with some very spicy punctuation. Renato had known Giulio from his college days. He had saved him many a reprimand, teaching him behavior and pride. Now Renato wanted Giulio to tell me some of his escapades. And after he told me some funny stories, we all laughed together. Giulio was turning red in the face with some of the stories being told, but he really was always a very well-behaved young man. I felt quite relieved and smiled approvingly at him.

It was planned that at noon we would stop at a sheep ranch in Italy. It was a small acreage and a small flock compared to the A-BAR-B. It was quite interesting to see the entire family of peasants as they milked the sheep and cows by hand. This milk was made into ricotta cheese on the ranch and sold directly from their ranch. A man or woman in the family would sit on a low stool and milk each ewe from behind—between the two hind legs. The ewe would walk away when the milking was done, and another would take its place. This had to be very time consuming and tiring for the family; but no one would complain. It was expected of them. This was the way they made their living.

Our refreshments were served outside—a tree stump for a table and the milking stools for our seats. We were treated with all the grace they could give nobility. They knew Renato and the Fiat car with its noble crest. A hand-embroidered cloth covered the tree stump for a tablecloth. We also had embroidered napkins and plain dishes with homegrown wheat, bread, and cookies. English tea was served in cups without saucers. Renato ate with their family. The mother and one of the sons waited on us. They were thrilled to know that I was an American bride. They were amused at my attempt of the Italian language. Giulio paid them with American money, which pleased them very much. This gave me a wonderful story to write to the A-BAR-B and for Father to tell all the cowboys and the cracker-box brigade—meaning our ranch hands and prairie friends.

On the rest of our trip to Berthamond, Giulio explained a bit to me about the estate. I had heard many stories before but was prepared to see and hear more. "Now my dear little North Dakota cowgirl, be prepared to see your castle that has stood on this mountainside since the Crusades," Giulio said.

Count Giulio de Sauteiron de St. Clement and his bride
Countess Dorothy Berry de St. Clement in Rome Italy – 1903

## This is Your Castle

"This is the Castella de Berthamond! It was built of stone and marble and stands in the foothills of the Alps as firm and as solid as the mountains themselves." And Giulio went on: "We will see it from the distance that it has become a part of the mountain itself.

"Dotty dear, down through the years, there have been earthquakes—some slight, some worse—but never a terrific opening up of the earth. This always means that these rumblings, moaning and groaning way down deep in the earth, cause some commotion above. Stones and gravel and sometimes a few rocks come rolling down until they find a lodging place. Oftentimes the castle, dear old Berthamond, has been the lodging place."

Giulio said, "Now be prepared, La Contessa Dorotea, the western side of this palazza is completely covered, absolutely covered, and this debris cannot be moved. Never has a window been broken. The wind still blows this sand and lava, and often the ground trembles, and perhaps someday it will become a part of the Alps. It has never bothered the inmates. Each generation has gone on and accepted the light and the dark rooms. You see, the estate of Berthamond is like a little village: the people live there and have their own homes. It is like our experiment stations here. They raise grapes and olives, and the income takes care of them. It is the old system, and it still works out with satisfaction. There is never a failure in crops as they put back in the ground the fertilizer needed, and it irrigates itself, if not enough rain falls.

"There are little cottages dotted all over this land, and they have their own vegetable and flower gardens. They have their own little chapel and their own Madonna, and a student priest comes here every Sunday. They also have a little theater, and they give their own plays and operas—tragedy and comedy. Sometimes they have outside talent. There is even a small orphan asylum, but it is seldom used.

"This old castle was given to our family, dating back to the Crusades at the same time the House of Savoy took over the kingdom. It has a wonderful history that we will read about together. There are four families or four branches, and they all live in this castle. Our family, de Sauteiron, has one apartment, which consists of twelve rooms. Now there are only little Mother left; Eugenia, Carlo's widow; you, Dorothy; and myself to occupy our twelve-room apartment. I am happy to tell you this, my darling. Our apartment is on the east side, and all our windows are open to let in the sunshine and air."

We were coming within sight of the castle now; a bend in the road brought it in full view as we came toward it from the south. I held my breath; it was so familiar, just as he described it. The whole panoramic view seemed so familiar, as if I had been here and had lived here before—as if I knew what I could not see. I had told Giulio this before when he had shown me the picture, and as he described it, I could add more to my mind. Tears were in my eyes as we came nearer. He would always add, "I believe you, Dotty, and when we arrive there, I know that you can prove it to me. Show me the way through the castle."

The picturesque roadway wound in and around the rough stones, and the long-sided slopes were rough and pebbly. Giulio was reminiscing: "Mother could never understand why Carlos, Guido, and I would wear out our woolen clothes; they would be hanging on us in tatters. We would walk up this slope as far as we could easily and then roll down. All of this lava gravel is so rough and so pointed, our clothes would really be so worn that they would drop off of us."

It was a beautiful time to see the silhouette of the castle. The sun was disappearing behind the foothills of the Alps. A gorgeous golden-red glow made the background for the gray stone medieval castle stand out in magnificent relief. Giulio was watching me and turning to look at the castle and again back to me. "Look closely, *mia contessina*. Is it your castle? Is it the same? Has it changed?"

It was my castle. It had been my home. I knew I felt that I had lived here before. I could not remember that any detail changed. I knew the castle outside and inside. The only change was that I had lived here before the landslides. I remembered the complete outline of all the turrets and a mountain outline behind that threw it in relief. I could see the inside of the castle. It was just as plain to me as the little ranch house on the A-BAR-B. There was a long, dark passageway on each floor where I could push a piece of paneling and the small door would open. Then down deep through a long dark tunnel, there was the last door, which had a spring to open it. That was the dungeon. I would show Giulio as soon as we entered; that was the proof of my dream world. I had lived here before.

We walked to the door; there were two massive bronze doors with carvings on them. Giulio handed me the giant-sized key. I could just manage to hold it. We were smiling into each other's eyes. Renato stood back with the suitcases in his hands. I put the key in so easily, and it turned with no effort. Giulio pushed the door gently with his foot, and it swung open. He then swooshed me right up into his arms and carried me across the threshold and put me down right in the center of the great hall. He made a low, slow bow and spoke to me in the sweetest Italian voice, "*Eccho la! La tua castella*! Welcome, La Contessa Dorotea de Sauteiron de St. Clement, my little American cowgirl! This is your Castle de Berthamond!"

Made in the USA
Columbia, SC
17 February 2020